What Can I Do?

What Can I Do?

A Handbook for Parents

By Tom Watson
Foreword by Nicky Cruz

Logos International
Plainfield, New Jersey

Unless otherwise identified, all scriptural quotations are from the *New English Bible* © Oxford University Press, 1970.

The Dedication

I should like to express my gratitude to my wife, Pat, for her endless retyping and for her helpfulness, without which my ministry would not have been possible. This volume is dedicated to her and to my three daughters—Lynn, Sherry, and Beth—who too often have had their meals interrupted by phone calls from troubled kids and who have understandingly told "Daddy" good-bye many times when he was called to respond to a crisis. For such a family, I can only echo the words of Chris Christopherson, "Why me, Lord?"

Foreword

Many times I have experienced a scared, shocked parent coming to me with the news, "My child's using drugs!" So often the parent is surprised, asking, "Why *my* child? What do I do now?" The mother or father feels he has let the child down, failed him in some way.

This book is for any parent whose teenager has used drugs. The author, Tom Watson, presents practical advice that is drawn from his years of experience in helping drug-using kids. He has insight into the problems of young people that few pastors, teachers, or psychiatrists have, because he has allowed himself to be personally involved with the families he has helped. Kids who use drugs are not just society's problem to him, they are his own.

It is because of his personal involvement that Tom is able to see the problems and the solutions so clearly.

Read this book, parents. I needed it. I think you do, too.

Nicky Cruz

Preface

Among the most painful memories of my ministry are those of parents who have sat in my office and told me the heartbreaking stories of what was happening in the lives of their children who had turned to drugs.

Probably no one feels more helpless than a mother or father whose son or daughter is on dope. "What should I do?" they ask.

During the last five years, I have dealt with that question hundreds of times. This book grew out of the cries for help by those pain-ridden souls.

The suggestions recorded here are not those of a psychiatrist or a psychologist. They are the answers I have received on my knees before the Lord. They are admittedly Christian and not "religious." I say that because so often parents have told me, "We want help for our child, but we just can't relate to religion."

Well, I have a hard time relating to "religion," too. But I have seen Jesus Christ transform the lives of many former drug addicts, and I have watched them become radiantly alive in the power of His Spirit.

If you are looking for answers other than in the abundant life Jesus promised, you will be disappointed by this volume—you might even find it offensive. However, if Jesus isn't the answer, I fear there is none. I have spent weeks at such places as Yale University's Drug Dependence Institute, The Synanon Foundation, and other programs run by the "experts." I have read volumes of studies and reports by the National Institute of Mental Health and other reputable agencies who are using the best of man's knowledge to help in the problem. I've watched kids transfer addiction from heroin to a new life-style, to transcendental meditation, to methadone, to alcohol, to sky-diving, and to group therapy. The results have been, at best, unsuccessful, and, at worst, destructive.

I am not a psychologist, or a medical doctor, or an expert. God called me out of a journalistic profession and has blessed me with a fruitful ministry among drug users and addicts. What I have learned, I wish to share with you. All of the experiences are real, but names have been changed and situations disguised to protect kids and their families.

Writing a book of this sort is an awesome thing because the writing carries with it the responsibility to pray for all who read it and for the loved ones for whom they are concerned. You have my pledge that I shall discharge that duty as long as the Lord gives me breath. Though I may never meet you, or your child, I shall daily lift your burden to the Lord in prayer.

Table of Contents

Chapter 1

Introduction

"Can You Come Down to the Station?"

"We got a phone call last night that shattered our world."

She was middle-aged, middle-class, an active church member, a good wife, a loving mother. I could almost see her in the kitchen baking cookies.

"Can you come down to the station, Mrs. Mitchell?" the sergeant had said. "Your son has been arrested on a charge of selling drugs."

"Robert's always been a good boy!" She started crying. "We've worked hard—tried to give him the things we didn't have." Now she was sobbing.

1

"I don't understand— Why us?" More tears.

"We go to church regularly— Robert did, too, until he started running around with that crowd. I teach a Sunday school class. . . . How can I ever face them again?"

"I know it hurts. Let it all come out," I said, trying to reassure her.

"The Bible says to train up a child in the way he should go, and when he is old, he won't depart from it. We've tried—really done our best—"

I knew she was right. Some of the most mixed-up kids I have seen come from beautiful Christian families. To be sure, broken homes and rotten parents are turning out drug addicts by the thousands, but we have to face the fact that some of the worst kids come from some of the "best" families.

"I feel like God has let us down," she continued, wiping her eyes with her handkerchief. "What's going to happen now?" she asked.

"Well, that depends, in large measure, on what you do now," I replied.

"What do you mean? I don't know what to do. I've never felt so helpless in my life! There are so many things to be decided. What should I tell the other children? What should we say to him? Should we bail him out of jail? Should we hire him a lawyer? What's going to happen to him at the trial? What about school?"

A brief talk with the person in jail often reveals how serious the problem really is.

"Pigs! That 'narc' had everybody believing he was our friend—"

"It wasn't even *my* dope. . . . A good lawyer can get this charge thrown out of court. . . . He set me up—it's a bum rap."

Pleas of guilty are hard to come by. Broken and contrite hearts are practically nonexistent among the defendants. Repentance? They never heard of it.

"Melinda's Run Away!"

There's another situation we often get called in on.

"Tom, Melinda's run away— After she left, we looked through her room and found some stuff that may be marijuana—and a whole bunch of pills," a father said.

"She left us a note that said 'I've got to find myself. Don't worry. . . . ' What does she mean, 'Don't worry'? She's only fifteen. . . . "

Every year, more than half a million kids leave parents with fears and hurts like these.

"I don't understand— We knew she'd been depressed lately—she'd missed a couple of days of school. . . . But we had no idea the situation was this bad."

There are the practical questions, like, "Should I call the police? Should we have the police question her friends? Should we go looking for her? But where in the world do you start looking? Should we talk to a psychiatrist?"

Then there are the more painful questions: "What makes a kid do that sort of thing? Does this mean we have failed our daughter? I've heard so much about drugs—you don't think she is an addict, do you? What if she's pregnant? What can we say to her when—and if—she comes back?"

The heart aches, the mind whirls, the spirit grieves.

No Easy Answers

There are no easy answers for complicated questions like those above. Probably the most damaging thing I could do would be to give you a list of easy steps to take. Every situation, every person is different. Every action must be weighed in the light of the total situation. In the final analysis, each parent must decide for himself.

The most helpful thing I can do is to focus on your role in the situation, discuss some of the reasons kids do dope, offer some suggestions as to how to bring the full redemptive power of God to work in the problem, and share some experiences I have had with parents and youths.

What follows is in that spirit. Please don't take this as "Watson's Law." I confess that one thing that has kept me from writing this book for more than a year has been the nightmare possibility of some parent holding such a book up to a kid and screaming, "Look what Tom Watson says about you!" If the thoughts contained in this book become the basis for some of your own convictions, I shall not feel the least slighted

5

if you use them without hinting where they have come from. Believe me, with kids, it's better that way.

Chapter 2

Why Do Kids Do Dope?

"Reverend, with all the publicity on the dangers and penalties of drug abuse, why do people get mixed up in this stuff?" a district court judge asked. He was about to pronounce sentence on a twenty-year-old boy who had pleaded guilty to possession of heroin. "I just don't understand it," he said.

For some, the "why" of drugs is an academic question, an interesting subject. But for a judge who cares, it is a plea for some justification for the mercy he feels when he faces young offenders.

For the parent who has just discovered that his youngster is into drugs, asking "Why" expresses the agony that has suddenly become his world. Sometimes it is

7

a way of saying, "Where did we go wrong?" or, "How did we fail?" or, "Everything I thought I knew suddenly means nothing."

And almost everybody has his answer to "Why?"

The sociologists talk about bad environmental situations, breakdowns in the family structure, emergence of new social mores, mobility, affluence, transience, and a host of other factors. All these factors probably have a lot of impact on the situation, but when your son or daughter is sitting in a jail cell, they don't offer either solace or direction.

Psychologists talk about the use of drugs as escape mechanisms, personal identity crises, and efforts at self-realization. While these factors certainly must be taken seriously, they only scratch the surface of the real reasons.

Spiritual Experience

Roger was a bright kid. In fact, he was too bright for the schools. Most of the time, he stayed bored with the subject matter and spent his time studying philosophy. While his peers were busy learning algebra and calculus, he was busy trying to improve on Einstein's theory of relativity.

Leaving school at the ripe old age of sixteen, Roger went out in search of the meaning of the universe. Soon he was into the peace movement, then into the drug culture.

Armed with a host of books by Abbie Hoffman, Timothy Leary, and other advocates of hallucinogenic drugs, he left home in search of "reality"—through peyote, LSD-25, and marijuana. Six months later, I visited him in a mental hospital where his condition was diagnosed as "acute schizophrenia."

Roger had been sure that he was finding the answers to the perplexing questions of life in psychedelic drugs, but now he clung to an empty cigarette package and told me it was his only point of contact with reality.

It is time we faced up to the fact that psychedelic drugs are a spiritual experience. Their effects often parallel experiences of great men and women in the Bible. Every claim I have ever heard for drugs has a counterpart in the New Testament.

Let's take a look at some of the claims of confirmed acid (LSD-25) users and their counterparts in Scripture:

"I felt like I was in touch with Ultimate Reality." Read Matthew 17:1-13. The transfiguration of Christ put Peter, James, and John in direct touch with *the* Reality.

"I saw vivid colors and patterns, heard strange sounds, and knew strange things." Read the Book of Revelation, especially the first chapter. Visions, strange sounds, insights into the unknown—it's all there.

"I felt like time and place had lost all significance." Read II Corinthians 12:1-9. When Paul was stoned (no pun intended) and left for dead at Lystra, he was caught up into the third heaven. Fourteen years later, he didn't even know whether or not he was "in the body."

"Everything was so intensely amplified." Read Acts 9:1-8. Saul's Damascus Road experience would probably be called a real "bummer."

"I felt like I was a part of everything around me." Wonder how Peter felt when he walked on the water? Matthew 14:22-23.

How do grass (marijuana) users feel? "It makes me feel good no matter how much of a hassle I'm in." Read Acts 16:16-30. Paul and Silas were beaten and thrown in jail. At midnight, with their backs bleeding, they "sang praises unto God." Sounds to me like they felt pretty good.

These are just a few of the drug-induced parallels or counterfeits of spiritual experiences that were the normal pattern for both the Old Testament prophets and the first-century Christians.

My encounters with hundreds of kids on everything from glue to cocaine indicates to me that the basic reason kids resort to drugs is their innate need for deep, personal, spiritual experience. They lack the real thing, so they are drawn to the counterfeit spiritual reality of drugs.

Some of us have become too sophisticated for miracles, visions, prophecies, or speaking in tongues, but we have not eliminated the needs they can satisfy from the lives of our children. They have turned to drugs, witchcraft, astrology, Satan worship, and meditation to find counterfeits.

In all my years of counseling, I have never met a kid on drugs who was not in search of some sort of spiritual reality, and I have never met a kid who had a vital, living relationship with God who found it necessary to do dope.

"But, Tom, I can't get my child to go to church." That is precisely what I am *not* talking about.

I stood in the educational plant of one of the largest churches in our city one Sunday morning a few minutes before eleven and listened to a sixteen-year-old girl plead with her parents not to make her go into "that thing in there."

I watched this girl go through marijuana, the psychedelics, and on to heroin during the next couple of years. It was only after she came into a real relationship with God that she was able to shake the drug habit.

Rock Music

Perhaps the best way to illustrate the Satanic counterfeit of spiritual experience is through a look into acid-rock music.

Whenever I am called into a home

where drug abuse is suspected, one of the first things I look at is the room of the youngster involved. Those way-out posters, strobe lights, incense burners, and acid-rock records may appear harmless, but in my experience, their presence indicates problems ahead for parents and child.

The following interview with a group of former drug abusers and addicts may help to explain:

Tom: Lanny, you once burned about $400 worth of albums—why?

Lanny: That's a hard question—because at the time, it was probably more something I felt than something I reasoned out.

But probably, one of the main reasons was that in those albums, the music—well, I could pull out any of those albums and listen, and it would take me back to a certain period in my past. Most of those albums I bought before I knew the Lord. It would just dig up parts of the old "me" that are dead now because I'm a new creature in Jesus. Most of the music represented the turmoil I went through before I met the Lord.

13

Tom: Karen, one night I was at Ken's house, and you called. You were in deep turmoil—you were bugged about albums. What were you going through that night?

Karen: Well, the Lord really told me to burn the albums. I didn't know why, because I felt like I could listen to them and still live in fellowship with the Lord.

But it kept on getting worse and worse, and I finally burned them—but there was still this thing about the spirit in one song. It would take me back, like it was possessing me. I was with a group of people one time, and this certain song came on the jukebox, and I just went away from myself, and I was in a completely different world from everybody else. It just dragged me back into my past. . . . I can't take that, because I don't want to live in that world anymore. It's dead and gone.

The night I sorted out my albums to be burned; I had them over in a corner. I woke up at four o'clock in the morning and looked over there, and there was a glowing light on those albums. I remembered that verse in the Bible about Satan coming as an angel of light. It was weird.

14

I knew then that they were not of the Lord and the only way I could get free from them was to let go of them.

After I burned them and my posters, I seemed to be able to flow into my room and not to walk into a brick wall like before when it was like spiritual forces battling at me every time I walked in there.

Tom: There are certain symbols that Christians have used over the centuries—the cross, for example. Are you saying that the forces of hell inhabit certain symbols of their own?

Karen: Definitely.

Tom: And you experienced that—a contact, through a physical representation, with a spiritual force?

Karen: Yes.

Lanny: I went to a concert about a year ago and there was a band— You wouldn't classify them as a Satanic group. They were a "Top 40" type group, really a tight band, really professional.

That was the night I was really convinced I could no longer be involved in rock music, because as the group was playing—and they were just doing nice "Top 40" type songs—the kids in that place, most of them fourteen to eighteen years old, were worked into a frenzy. They were all around the stage—dancing and on each others' shoulders. It was beginning to look like an orgy right there in the coliseum.

I looked on the stage and saw this horrible creature standing there dancing. I just knew it was a demon. That was what I needed to let me know that that music is definitely of Satan.

Tom: Ken, you have played professionally. What does it feel like, as a musician, to get a group of kids worked into a wild frenzy?

Ken: It really makes you feel like you've got the same powers that God has.

Tom: When you really get into it, what does it feel like?

Ken: Well, one of the top songs we did was "God Damn the Pusher." After I was saved, I was really wondering if I could stay with the band. One night a girl came up and asked me to play that song. As I looked at her, I saw my little five-year-old daughter's face. It was as if this girl could be my own daughter.

My foul tongue had just been taken away by the Lord, and I had friends who were pushers. I didn't know whether the song was saying "God damn the pusher" or "God, *You* damn the pusher," but I realized I couldn't go along with either way. I couldn't use the Lord's name in vain, and I didn't want God to damn my friends. I just couldn't play it that night.

You talk about an awful feeling— Stand up in front of people and try to fake rock music. You can't fake rock music. If you're not into it, you can't fake it, that's all there is to it.

Tom: It's got to express what's really inside of you?

Ken: That's right! And, that's the reason people say, "This is real." It *is* real. It *has* to be real.

We used to go to a place to play, and we would say, "Are we going to play soul music because it's a booze crowd or rock music because it's a dope crowd?"

Gary: When I started playing rock bands, I was supposedly a Christian. I was a very calm person when I was off-stage. I was very quiet. I didn't drink, or curse, or smoke—I didn't do nothing.

But as soon as I hit that stage, I would take out all my violence and frustrations in the music I played. What was really deep inside came out in my playing the drums.

The more I took out my frustrations, the wilder the crowd got.

Tom: You were giving expression to what they felt inside?

Gary: That's right.

Tom: Where does the name "acid-rock" come from?

Billy: I read somewhere—and this was true for me—that acid-rock was associated with dope because it recreated for a "non-tripping" listener what a "tripping" listener heard when he was "tripping." This is done through distortion on a guitar and strobe lights and Leslies and stuff like that.

When you're using acid, you can do whatever you want to do with your head. The music will help you with the trip.

Tom: Did any of you ever feel like you were helping people get into dope?

Gary: Yeah! It really tore me up. People would walk up to me with a bag of dope or whatever— You find that you are helping these people kill themselves, spiritually and physically.

Like, they'd walk up to me and say, "Hurry up and play—I've gotta have a lift, man. I can't do it without your music."

I was being used. It took me a long time to realize what I was doing to people—I was killing them, just through the music I was playing. When I found out I was killing people, it tore me to pieces.

Scott Nixon: I used to handle equipment for a group. Once we went to a university for a whole weekend to play for a fraternity. It was "Imp Weekend." I saw about thirty or forty guys dressed up like Satan coming across a bridge. I was wondering what was happening.

The next day, we were playing, and there was another band across the street. We were seeing who could be the loudest, and that kind of stuff.

The people started having a mud fight—heaving mud over on our equipment. I was getting pretty upset about it. And I was sitting there when I felt something sprinkling from the house. I looked up, and there was a guy urinating on me.

The music, the crowd, the people rolling around in the mud, and the beer were turning our future leaders of America into pigs on the ground, having wild pig orgies. They were so wrapped up in this thing—the music, the beer, and

"This is the cool thing to do." I just had to get out of there.

Tom: What about a typical kid listening to rock records in his room?

Barbara: I've never been into rock music like all these other people. But, I've seen the effect of all this on some people I love.

What really hit me the deepest was my brother. I came home after being away at school. . . . When he would get into down moods, he would go into his room and shut the door and listen to the music. When I came home, I found him lying on the bed like a zombie.

I said, "What in the world are you doing?" He had been playing this one record over and over and over. I don't know how long he'd been listening to it.

And he said, "I don't want to live!" Now, my brother is not a depressed person. I don't know what the music did to him, but I know it wasn't good.

It's like it transfers an emotion. I was into folk music, and the thing I always wanted to get across to people was a feeling—whatever emotion the song was trying to convey, that's what I wanted to put on the people.

I was giving people frustration, because I was making them have all these bad feelings, and I didn't give them any answers. But I meant well.

Tom: The Bible talks about Satan coming to people as a wolf in sheep's clothing. Isn't this what we are talking about?

Barbara: I can really see the wolf in sheep's clothing, because I would sing these songs out of a concern for the problem. I'd want people to see it and do something about it. And yet, it was like running around in circles—it just led right back to the frustration of not having any solution.

Lanny: In a way, I praise God for what I went through in music, because the search that music led me through is what brought me to Jesus. It doesn't do any good just to say to people who aren't born-again Christians, "Look, rock music is bad. Get out of it." But they listen when I give my personal testimony of how the Lord brought me out of all of that.

. Now don't jump to the conclusion that I am suggesting, "Rid your child of rock music and all the accouterments and his drug problem will be solved." Not at all. Drugs are a spiritual experience, and until his spiritual hunger is satisfied, a person will keep on seeking for a way to fill the void in his life.

Peer Group Pressure

"Everything was all right until he started running around with that crowd," is a typical comment from a troubled parent.

It is easy to see *how* a crowd of dopeheads has influenced a person's behavior. It is often not so easy to see *why*.

The *why* starts in the cradle, with television. One mother told me recently that if it were not for cartoons on Saturday morning, she would not be able to survive the weekend with her small children. If you don't think television forces kids to identify with their peers, just take a look at the toys they want when Christmas rolls around—or the cereals they want you to get from the grocery store.

Then come the school years, and a whole new emphasis. By the time a child is six, often much earlier, he is forced to seek identity outside the home—with his peers. Long before junior high school, a child's primary personal identity is outside the home. No wonder the home has little influence on his behavior patterns by the time he is a teenager.

Even the church works to separate the family. When a family goes to Sunday school, they split in as many directions as there are family members. And when they come together for morning worship, it is in a place where the children's feet dangle in space. The whole worship service is geared to an adult audience, and the primary message the children get is, "Sit still, look straight ahead, be quiet."

Every major study done in recent years points up that the greatest single desire of a teenager is to be accepted by his peers. A person cannot stand to be outside a circle. If he cannot find acceptance in one circle, he will seek out another.

Acceptance—Anywhere

Often a youngster feels outside those groups in which he wants to find acceptance. At home he is "hassled" about his hair, his music, his irresponsibility, his dirty room, his clothes, his lack of industry, his grades, etc. He looks for acceptance elsewhere.

Quite often a teenager cannot compete satisfactorily with his peers in school situations. His problem may be that of not being able to read well. So he turns to role playing. He may become the clown, the rebel, the group scapegoat. More "hassles." Again, he is on the outside looking in.

The dope crowd is pretty liberal about accepting outsiders. The only person rejected is the "narc," or "pig." Once convinced that a person is not on the side of the law, the dopers accept him. And since there are no other circles open to the outsider, he settles for whatever status he might achieve with the dope crowd. Sometimes he gains recognition by doing more bizarre things than anyone else in the group. If he buys dope, he is a customer, and therefore needed by the dealer. If he sells dope, he is a source, and therefore needed by the users. For many, involvement with dope is identified with the first time in their lives they have felt accepted or needed by anybody.

I have talked with girls who would die for some guy who treated them like dirt, simply because "He needs me." You almost have to be in this culture to understand why a girl will risk prison, sell her body, or lie for a guy who sleeps with her and then steals everything she has to sell for money for dope. One drug addict I knew was physically dissipated to the point of being repulsive to look at. He stole from everybody, lied when the truth would have served him better, and yet, at one point, he had six girls trying to kill each other over him. Four of the girls explained, "He needs me."

Dr. Harold Glasser, in his book, *Reality Therapy*, says that every person needs basically two things. He needs to love and to be loved, and to have the feeling that he is a worthwhile person.

Victor Frankl, an Austrian psychiatrist, in his book, *Logotherapy, Man's Search for Meaning*, says that man's most basic drive is his desire for personal meaning. "Who am I?" is the basic question at the root of the identity struggles and the reason for all the peer group pressure. This may be explained psychologically, but basically, it is a spiritual problem. In a later book, *The Doctor and the Soul*, Dr. Frankl says that many of the problems with which psychiatrists deal should be referred to the minister. In other words, they are spiritual problems.

When a person comes into a living relationship with God, there is available to him a fantastic feeling of acceptance. After you are accepted by the Sovereign of the universe, and really accept that acceptance, rejection by men is no longer the ominous monster it once was.

When a person comes to accept the authority of God, he is no longer motivated to "do his own thing." He wants to know and do the will of God. And in this, all of his basic needs are met. He is loved, he loves, he feels worthwhile, and he finds that ultimate meaning for himself is to live in union and fellowship with the God Who created him and Who died for him.

In Christ, a person can never be on the outside of the body of believers. Christ brings union with God and with man. Once a person has a taste of this belonging, he can never be satisfied with anything less.

Solve the Spiritual Problem— Solve the Drug Problem

In the final analysis, if you can solve the spiritual problem, the drug problem will take care of itself.

A person can be cured of the physical effects of even heroin within a period of seventy-two hours. Some have been instantly and miraculously delivered from mammoth drug habits through the laying on of hands and prayer.

When a person experiences a "new birth" in Christ, his whole outlook on life changes. He is given the life of Christ, and his dominant desire is to respond to the newness within him. It is no longer a matter of talking him into more acceptable behavior or getting him to act more maturely; he is a new creature in Christ Jesus. Once a person has accepted Jesus as his Lord, all he needs is nurture to grow into full spiritual and emotional maturity.

The same thing that draws a person into drugs—seeking for spiritual reality— makes him a beautiful person once he has found a real relationship with God. When a person comes from the agonizing depths of drug addiction, he already

27

knows what hell is like, and he wants a
taste of heaven.

Chapter 3

The Parents' Role

"Tom, can you get over here right away? We're in big trouble with our son!"

I dropped everything and rushed over to her home to find her pacing the floor. She was frantic; her husband appeared stunned.

She handed me a little brown paper bag. "We think it's marijuana—we found it in the ashtray of the family car after Joe used it last night— Oh, what are we going to do?"

I opened the bag. Inside was a piece of tinfoil; inside that was a piece of plastic wrap; inside that was the "bogey."

"What's the best institution in the country? Money is no object. We want

the best care for our son," the father
said.

I felt like asking them what kind of
flowers they wanted for the boy's fu-
neral.

"Looks like rolled up tea leaves to me.
Let's have it analyzed," I suggested.
The result showed "no illegal drug
content."

Over-reaction is probably the most
common error of parents who suspect or
find out for sure their youngster is in
trouble with drugs. Suddenly, he is no
longer their child who has needs and is
looking for answers to the dilemma of
his life. He is like a leper or a raving
maniac, a monster to be feared.

What Kind of Help?

Psychiatry

There are certain solutions parents
usually think of at the first sign of a drug
problem.

"Let's take Johnny to a psychiatrist
and get him straightened out," a parent
says.

Unfortunately, it doesn't work that way. Psychoanalysis requires intense desire on the part of the patient, and no teenager who has been "taken to a shrink" is going to put forth the effort. He is usually convinced that the problem is not his anyway.

Furthermore, very few psychiatrists are equipped to deal with drug problems, as such. I have attended seminars with psychiatrists who quite frankly admitted they were at a loss to deal with the drug problem. In five years of ministry to troubled youth, I have never seen a drug addict cured by a psychiatrist or psychiatric clinic. Mental health centers have been able to provide support services, such as group therapy, which have helped hold some habits in check, but their effectiveness has generally been limited.

Several things bother me about the psychiatric approach to the problem. Many times drugs are prescribed to help the youngster. One girl I knew who was struggling out of a "downer" habit went to a psychiatrist who, on the first visit, gave her a prescription for tranquilizers. She took all the pills, had a ball, and never went back. Almost every kid we have dealt with who has seen a psychiatrist has been given pills of some sort. A prescription for pills just compounds the problem.

Another difficulty is that most teenagers misinterpret the "acceptance" by their counselor as permissiveness and sometimes even as an endorsement of their behavior. People with drug problems, regardless of what they say, want to be led. If counselors don't lead them, their friends will.

Perhaps the most serious problem we have encountered in referring kids to psychiatrists is that non-Christian psychiatrists often seek to rid a person of his "religious conflicts" by assuring him that all this business about God is a carry-over from the dark ages. A Spirit-filled Christian psychiatrist can be a real help in assisting a youngster to find the real meaning of life and the source of his conflict, but an atheist psychiatrist can do more damage in a few visits than you can straighten out in a lifetime.

Finally, that one-hour-a-week visit is not going to provide the support a person needs to deal with all the conflicts reflected by his drug problem.

These comments should not be taken

as a criticism of psychiatrists. They are, rather, an effort to diminish the unrealistic expectations most parents have when they turn to psychiatry for help with a drug problem.

Drug Programs

Where drug programs are available, people turn to them for help and are often disillusioned. A key man on the staff of Yale University's Drug Dependence Institute told us once in a seminar that their research indicated that a twelve to fifteen percent effectiveness ratio was good, and that most governmental programs operated in the range of a five to ten percent cure rate for drug addiction.

Methadone and the drug antagonist programs are the greatest farces of all. I say this as one who has tried. For seven months we operated a federally funded methadone detoxification program only to find that we were providing people with nothing more than a rest from the hassle of trying to find heroin. Usually, before they even completed the program, the addicts we treated were back on the streets.

Synanon and similar programs often claim a much higher ratio of "cures" among those who complete the program. What they don't tell you is that sixty to eighty percent of those taken in "split" within the first week. Others don't make it through the first month.

Christian Rehabilitation Facilities

A number of Christian rehabilitation facilities are in operation and are doing a good job of reclaiming drug addicts. Teen Challenge, Nicky Cruz Outreach, Inc., and several others are based on the same principles I am offering in this book. If you can get your child into such a center, he may receive the love and nurture he needs to fight his way back from addiction.

It should be noted, however, that not all agencies that call themselves Christian are effective in dealing with the problems of drug users. I would suggest that you visit a center and talk to some of the people in the program before you enroll a youngster for help.

Prison

Another alternative to curb a drug problem is to send the young addict to prison. Sometimes a judge has no choice other than to impose an active sentence, but in most cases, this only compounds the problem. Drugs are usually available in the prison or reformatory.

Prison may be necessary as a deterrent to the habitual drug user and pusher, but its rehabilitative capability is practically nil. Sometimes serving a jail sentence can start a person thinking about his needs, but this rarely happens unless peripheral counseling services are offered.

Ministers

The best source of help available to parents of delinquent teens may be the local minister. Sadly, he is usually the last person to find out about the problem. One of the leading ministers in our city told a drug task force that in twenty-five years of pastoring, he had never been approached by a person or family with drug problems. At that time, I was dealing with three families in his church who were victims of the chemical monster.

Many parents who come to me say that they have gotten no help from their church. Asked if they ever talked to the pastor about it, they say, "We thought he already knew about it," or "He's supposed to know these things!" If you don't tell your pastor about your youngster's drug problem, he may never know. If he does know, your silence indicates he would be intruding if he came to you.

Other parents don't want the minister or church leaders to know their child is in trouble. "Before I tell you who I am, you have to give me your word that you won't tell my minister, or anyone from my church about our problem," a mother once said to me on the phone. "I'd be embarrassed to death if they ever found out," she added.

"I think you are wrong in trying to hide this situation from your minister," I replied. "He, and the people of your church, would be glad to help. After all, what is a Christian fellowship for? If you find anything but warmth and concern from your church, you need a new church."

This mother was in for a pleasant surprise. Her minister was not able to help her son much, but he was a real lifesaver to her and her husband. She found that there were other parents in the church who were going through the same thing. They started going to a prayer group from which they drew much strength, and this strength gave them a firm foundation from which to help their boy.

Charity Begins at Home

You can probably do more than anyone else to supply the help your youngster needs. With the right attitude and actions, you can achieve a great deal.

Before we examine your role, let's take a look at what your role is *not*.

A Doormat: One thing your son or daughter needs to hear from you right away is that, although you love him, you are not going to permit him to walk all over you and the other members of the family. People who get into drugs often develop an exaggerated view of themselves, and their ego demands the restructuring of all the lives they touch.

Many parents I have dealt with live in terror. "If I tell her to do something she doesn't want to do, she'll leave," one mother said.

Not only does the doormat approach create a hell on earth for the family, it is terribly damaging and disorienting to the teenager.

One father I know handled this problem quite well when his sixteen-year-old daughter called him from a distant city after running away the day before.

"Last night mother and I were pretty upset—we were heartbroken. We miss you and are concerned about you," he said. "But this morning, I went to work, mother went to her Bible study, and your brother went on to school. We want you to be a part of our lives, but if you choose not to, then we will have to go on without you. Our world is not going to end just because you walk out of it."

A teenager needs to know that he is loved and needed, but it is a dangerous thing for him to get the impression that he is the center of your world. Once he feels that, he will seek to manipulate you, resulting in misery for you and destruction for him.

"We'd love for you to come back—we'll

even send you airplane fare," the father continued, "but in order to rejoin the family, you'll have to agree to some ground rules. When you get home we will sit down and talk about it, and if you think we are unfair or arbitrary, you always have the option to leave again." The girl agreed to return home and to give the rules a try.

On this foundation, the stage was set for her recovery. During the next two years, the daughter pushed at her restraints, often just to test the limits, but recently she has started doing much better.

A Preacher: Most teenagers who are into dope live with terrible feelings of guilt. This guilt expresses itself as anger—particularly toward those whom he loves most. The teen is condemned already by his conscience. He is not about to sit still and listen to a parent preach to him about his sins.

He is also living with so much fear that he has to have defense mechanisms to survive. The more you try to talk about the harmful effects of drugs, the more he is likely to tune you out.

"But shouldn't I warn him about the

dangers involved?" you ask. The time when you could warn him, and should have warned him, has already passed. At this stage in his life, he is convinced you don't know much. He may even be proud of the fact that he already knows more about drugs than you'll ever know—however erroneous his information.

People don't start using drugs for intellectual reasons, nor do they stop using them for intellectual reasons. The problem is spiritual. When something happens to change his life, he will quit. You will never be able to preach him into it.

"Should I just stand silently by and watch him kill himself?" I almost hear you exclaim. Indeed not, but preaching is not the effective way to deal with his needs. The young person is in rebellion against God, and you are a part of what he is rebelling against. When he makes his peace with God, he will submit to you.

You can be sure that God is already dealing with him much more effectively than you ever could. Almost everything he sees outside his drug culture is a condemnation to him, without you saying a word.

The end result is what you are looking for. Therefore, the method—in this case preaching—has to be evaluated on the basis of what comes back, not what goes out. If the end result of your efforts at preaching is hostility and rejection, it seems logical to try a different approach. Leave the preaching to those vessels whom God chooses.

Savior: Much as you want to, you cannot save your child from the grip of Satan. This is a work of the Holy Spirit. It is a work only He can do.

If you get so caught up in fear that you become frantic about your child, everything you have ever told him about the peace you have found in God will come across to him as a lie. If you are popping tranquilizers to keep calm, you are in no position to talk to your "pothead" son or daughter about what God can do in his life.

Your child has the freedom to choose whether he will destroy his life or come to peace with God. You can influence greatly his decision in ways that we will discuss later, but you cannot save him yourself. In fact, your efforts to rescue him may only delay, or possibly, even prevent, his encounter with the only real Savior—Jesus Christ.

If your youngster does not need you to be a doormat, a preacher, or a savior, what does he need from you?

Your Role

Recently I sat in my living room during a tremendous storm. Lightning was banging all around, thunder was rolling, the wind was blowing furiously. Soon, my three children had transferred their activities to the room where I was sitting.

Suddenly a bolt of lightning hit a tree just outside. Instantly, three sets of eyes jerked toward me. They wanted to see how I would react to what appeared to them a desperate situation. In the same way, a drug-addicted child watches his parents and can be helped or hindered by their reactions.

Tower of Strength: As hard as it may be to believe, with all his pronouncements to the contrary, your child is lost, frightened, guilt-ridden, lonely. Can he turn to you for help?

A girl told me this week that she was terrified at the prospect of talking to her mother about her involvement in drugs. She was not afraid to incur her mother's wrath. She was not afraid her mother would turn her over to the police, since it had been months since she had done drugs. What did she fear?

"If I tell her, she will come apart at the seams," she said, adding, "My mother is a very weak person."

One night, Ed Spivey, a friend who has helped countless drug abusers in our city while working with Contact, a telephone ministry, took a fourteen-year-old girl home well after midnight. The police had offered this as an alternative to sending the girl to a detention home.

"You're on drugs?" her mother screamed when they arrived at the door. "What will my friends say? How can I ever hold my head up at the club?" In this critical moment, mother failed the test, and her failure contributed to the serious turn of events that followed.

To be a parent, especially in a drug crisis, requires a great deal of poise and strength, more strength, in fact, than you can probably muster on your own. If you feel that you are about to "come unglued," you had better find a source of strength that can give you the power to stand.

A lot of parents talk to me about their faith in God, but very few of them exhibit the faith and peace that are spoken of in the Bible among the fruits of the Spirit (Gal. 5:22-23). But it is possible to do so. And as you demonstrate that your relationship with Christ produces love, joy, peace, longsuffering, hope, and faith in the midst of a drug crisis, your example will be more powerful than anything you or anyone else can say to your child about the power of God to meet the needs of his own life.

One father told me, "I'm not going to let this situation with my daughter defeat me. I have found a lot of comfort in the Holy Spirit, and I'm convinced there is even more there for me."

His daughter's reaction to his faith was, "My daddy's faith through all of this has amazed me. I know I have put him through hell, but he has never lost his serenity. In fact, it seems to be growing." Her conclusion was beautiful. "I hope some day I can come to know God like that."

Acceptance: People who do dope are looking for acceptance. It is very important that you accept your child as he is to avoid chasing him further into rebellion, but it is equally important that you maintain your own values.

Now, this may sound like a paradox, but it can be done. It may be expressed as follows: "We will always love you, no matter what you do. You will always be our son (daughter). But, as long as you live here, you will respect our values as we will try to respect yours. If there is any rejecting to be done, it will be done by you."

Perhaps it is more important to feel this than it is to say it. With God's help, it is possible to accept a person while rejecting his actions. A good example is the way Jesus handled the situation of the woman taken in adultery. He said to her, "Nor do I condemn you. You may go; do not sin again" (John 8:1-11).

The story is told of three boys in the nineteenth century who were kicked out of an ivy league college for pitching a big drunk. Their parents were notified by telegraph, and all responded immediately.

"You have disgraced us. Don't come home," said the first message to arrive from home.

"How could you, after all we have done for you?" said the wire from the parents of the second boy.

The third boy's father sent a wire which said simply, "Steady, boy, steady."

Isn't this what real love is all about?

Confidence: In one of the most turbulent periods of my life, a friend looked at me and said softly, "Tom, I believe in you."

I don't think I shall ever be able to express what that meant to me at the time and many times since then.

Many kids who are into drugs tell me, "Everybody is down on me."

"I know you're going to make it," a friend told his son, even though the boy was shooting heroin. An even more beautiful thing is that he told me privately, "And, you know, I believe he will."

Every teenager on drugs feels that it is a temporary state of affairs and that someday he is going to shake it. Your expression of confidence in your child and in the power of God may help more than you will ever know.

Channel of God's love: Perhaps your most important role is to provide a channel through which God's love can flow into the life of your troubled youngster.

Chapter 4

The Power of God's Love

When all of the best of men's devices fail, God's transforming power stands ready, eager to work its miraculous intervention in the hopeless mess drugs have made of a life. The only force in the world that can lift a person from the damning clutches of a drug habit to the thrilling experience of abundant life is the love of Jesus.

"In talking to you about love, I shall not get mushy and sentimental," says Starr Daily. "Love is everything that sentimentalism is not. Love is power, while sentimentalism is the misuse of power. Love is the only integrating power in existence. It is all that can establish order out of chaos or maintain order in chaos. Wherever it is recognized by man, he likewise recognizes harmony. Love is never a disintegrating force" (*Love Can Open Prison Doors*).

The above words were penned by a man who, after being diagnosed a hopeless criminal, came in contact with the redeeming power of God's love. No matter how hopeless your situation now seems, the power of God's love can bring order from the chaos, glory from the agony, beauty from the misery.

Ellen was fifteen when we first encountered her. She was attractive, bright, talented—insecure, angry, lonely. At a very early age, she had lost her father. Her mother had resigned herself to the fate of rearing her children alone. A feeling of gloom and despair pervaded their poorly furnished home.

Then, along came Bert. He was twenty-one, handsome, separated from his wife. He was a compulsive thief and liar, an alcoholic, a dope fiend, a suicidal maniac. His life was the very expression of the feelings that were beginning to stir within Ellen.

She got into dope and sex with him and his friends. Soon, she ran away with him, but their time together was short-lived. The police had been looking for him for a long list of crimes. Bert landed in jail, and Ellen was returned to her home.

When her lover committed suicide after being sent to a mental hospital, Ellen felt as if her world had come to an end. I, and some friends, began to pray that God's love would break through Ellen's despair. Finally, at the point of suicide herself, she came looking for me.

"I've got to have some answers!" she blurted out. "I can't go on any further!"

"Ellen, Jesus loves you and wants to make your life more beautiful than you could ever imagine," I told her.

She reacted violently, cursing her family, God, Who had taken her father and Bert, and the cruel people who were always taking advantage of her mother. The hatred that spewed out of her was enough to kill anyone. Yet I felt no condemnation toward her. I felt only hurt for the emptiness of her life. When she was finished, the Lord spoke to her through me.

"Ellen, Jesus loves you," I began, sharing how Jesus had died for her and that the Holy Spirit wanted to give her love, joy, peace. She sat silently for a long time. I knew I had done all I could do, so I just silently prayed in the Spirit.

Suddenly, a smile broke on her face.

"He loves me," she said. At first it was almost a whisper.

"He loves me."

"He loves me!" It became a shout.

For thirty minutes, that's all she could say, over and over again. Was this an emotional experience? Of course, but the days, and years, that followed indicated that something deeper had taken place as well. The Holy Spirit had brought the full power of God's love into play and had transformed her life. Ellen is now happily married to a fine Christian man. At this writing, five years after her "experience," she is excitedly expecting her first child.

I have watched this transformation happen many times, in many persons. People who hated their parents, the police, the system—everything—have burst into a song of joy and love in response to prayer and the message that Jesus loves them. It is the power of God at work.

One of the most difficult things for parents to accept is that God loves their

children more than they could ever love
them.

Whither shall I go from thy Spirit?
or whither shall I flee from thy
        presence?
If I ascend up into heaven, thou art
        there:
If I make my bed in hell, behold,
        thou art there.
If I take the wings of the morning,
and dwell in the uttermost parts of
        the sea;
Even there shall thy hand lead me,
and thy right hand shall hold me.
If I say, Surely the darkness shall
        cover me;
even the night shall be light about
        me;
Yea, the darkness hideth not from
        thee;
but the night shineth as the day:
the darkness and the light are both
        alike to thee.
For thou hast possessed my reins:
thou hast covered me in my moth-
        er's womb.
                        Psalm 139:7-13 (KJV)
We have a tendency to interpret this
Scripture in the framework that says,
"Jehovah's gonna' get you, if you don't

watch out." But how far from that the Psalmist was when he says a few verses later, "How precious also are thy thoughts unto me, O God! how great is the sum of them!"

The concept of God's grace is more than we can comprehend. When Jesus hung on the cross two thousand years ago, He knew where your child would be today. And it was precisely because of that knowledge that He died. Every thought of His mind is one of redemption toward us.

Our prayers do not try to talk God into doing something He does not want to do, but rather, to bring our will into union with His great purposes so that He can accomplish what He wants to do in us and for us.

"It is not his will for any to be lost, but for all to come to repentance," according to II Peter 3:9.

"All of this is well and good," said one mother to me, "but my son has to go to court next Wednesday. Facts are facts! You can't live in a dream world and spend all your time thinking about what you want God to do and what He wants to do."

One of Satan's craftiest tricks is to get

us to focus our attention on a set of facts, which he carefully chooses, and to believe that they comprise the whole picture. When he is able to get us into this trap, all we can see are those facts that drive us to despair and hopelessness.

There is an interesting story in II Kings 6:8-23. The prophet, Elisha, was being used so effectively by God that the king of Syria decided that he must be killed. So he sent an army down to Dothan to capture him. Silently, in the night, the troops closed in on the hills around the little village.

Early the next morning, Elisha's servant went out to look around, and he saw the massive hosts of horses, chariots, and horsemen. Immediately, he knew why they were there. In panic, he ran back into the tent and told Elisha what he has seen.

"Oh, master," he said, "which way are we to turn?"

"Do not be afraid," the old prophet replied, "for those who are on our side are more than those on theirs." Then he prayed for his servant: "O Lord, open his eyes and let him see."

The Lord opened the servant's eyes, and when he looked back he saw, not only the horses and chariots of the enemy, but also horses and chariots of fire, God's angels, ready to protect the prophet.

He had seen the "facts," but, when God opened his eyes, he saw the facts as God saw them, and as Elisha, through the eyes of the Spirit, saw them. There was nothing to be worried about. There would be a battle but no massacre.

Facts are facts, but any presentation of the facts that does not include the presence of God's redemptive love is only half the truth, or a whole lie.

If you are caught up in the despair of the immediate situation, my prayer for you is that God will open your eyes so that you can see that God is still in control, and is working all things together for good.

Matthew 14:22-33 tells how Jesus came walking on the stormy sea toward His disciples who were in a little boat that was about to sink.

"Take heart! It is I; do not be afraid," He said to them. He saw beyond the storm.

"Lord, if it is you, tell me to come to you over the water," Peter said. And Jesus told him to come.

Over the side of the boat he went, the water became solid beneath his feet, and he started walking toward Jesus. Everything was all right as long as he kept his eyes on Jesus.

"But when he saw the strength of the gale, he was seized with fear; and beginning to sink, he cried, 'Save me, Lord.'"

"Jesus at once reached out and caught hold of him, and said, 'Why did you hesitate? How little faith you have!' They then climbed into the boat; and the wind dropped. And the men in the boat fell at his feet, exclaiming, 'Truly you are the Son of God.'"

When Jesus comes on the scene, everything is changed. Despair becomes hope, fear becomes trust, anguish becomes peace.

I am not suggesting that there is no danger. Faith is not, as someone suggested, "Believing what you know ain't so anyhow." Faith is not the denial of danger, or calamity, or pain. Faith is the affirmation of the presence and power of God to deal with the situation, no matter how bad it is. It is not the absence of the forces of hell, but, rather, the presence of the forces of heaven.

57

Jesus' promise of "abundant life," and "rivers of living water" flowing out of our innermost being was not in any way conditional on the right kind of situation.

Jesus said that His Gospel was to the poor, the downcast, the brokenhearted, the captives, the blind, the bruised. He said those who were whole had no need of His healing, but those who were sick.

Men cannot "lift themselves by their own bootstraps." The whole concept of the Sermon on the Mount is based on poverty of spirit—an awareness of our total dependence on God to lift us out of the depths of despair and into the realms of glory.

Chapter 5

How to Tap the
River of Living Water

You can do more than anyone to bring your child into the full stream of God's redeeming love, but first, you have to tap that river of living water for yourself.

When I am called into a family situation involving drugs, I attempt to determine who is actually hurting. Interestingly, it is most often the parents or other members of the family who are smarting under the strain. Usually the child on drugs is insulated enough by the drugs and other elements of his culture that he is wondering why everybody is so upset. Thus, a great deal of ministry has to be directed to parents. Once they meet Christ and experience His love, they can play a leading role in bringing healing to the troubled kid. Until that happens, any healing for the child is going to be difficult to obtain.

What we are talking about is life—new life, real life, life in the Spirit. You can impart that life to your child and others, but you must have it yourself to do so. After all, a dead man or a dead woman cannot conceive life in the flesh. It makes sense that only those who are alive in the Holy Spirit can transmit His life to those who are dead in trespasses and sin.

Many of the parents I see want to bargain with God, or make a contract for Him to deliver certain services for which they will seek to repay Him. Parents quite often tell me they have prayed diligently for God to deliver a person from the grip of drugs but, "Nothing's happened."

"Have you drunk freely of the fountain of life yourself?" I ask.

"Look," they reply, "I'm not thinking about myself just now. All I can think about is God getting my child out of this mess." They want God to use them as an empty pipe through which His love can flow, but they don't want any of the residue to rub off on them.

My experience has been that it doesn't work that way. God's intervention in a crisis actually could better be compared to a bucket into which His love and life flow. When the bucket gets full, it overflows, and it is this spillage that is used in ministry to others.

When Jesus described the person who believed in Him, He said, "Streams of living water shall flow out from within him" (John 7:38). He was quite emphatic in His teaching that it is not what goes into a man that counts but what comes out. "The words that the mouth utters come from the overflowing of the heart" (Matt. 12:34).

Jesus promised that He would do anything we asked—but He laid down a condition for the fulfillment of that promise: "If you dwell in me, and my words dwell in you, ask what you will, and you shall have it" (John 15:7). In the same chapter of John, Jesus talks about man's relationship with Him: "I am the vine, and you are the branches" (John 15:5). It is only as the branch is united to the vine that it can draw the necessary life and bring forth fruit.

Right now, you might be near the point of panic. You might be desperate enough for God to perform the miracle you need. If so, you're ready for the first step in "plugging into life."

1. *Admit your helplessness before God.* I worked with one mother for more than a year during which she "tried everything." The more she did, the more the problem increased, until she and her daughter finally reached an impasse and the girl left home with a boyfriend. Months went by, and I heard nothing from the family until one night the mother called me.

"Tom, Ann came home about four weeks ago. She is like a different person," she told me. "She has a beautiful attitude—she talks to us. For the first time in years, she is a part of the family."

"What happened to bring about the change?" I asked.

"Well, when she left that last time, I just admitted that I could do nothing and turned it over to God," the mother replied, adding, "He worked it out in a way I never could have."

When a crisis of great magnitude hits your home, and there is no human who can deal with it, you need help from

God. He will work miracles when you really turn it over to Him.

2. *Ask God to fill you with His Holy Spirit.* If it is true that drugs are a counterfeit spiritual experience, you are dealing with a power far beyond your abilities.

John the Baptist promised that Jesus would baptize with the Holy Spirit those who followed Him. And Jesus told His disciples, "I am with you now, but I shall be in you." Jesus, through the Holy Spirit, can reproduce Himself in you.

Several key words stand out in a study of Jesus' promises regarding the Holy Spirit.

Power: Jesus promised that through the indwelling of the Holy Spirit we would receive power. This means that through Him we can experience the same power that raised Jesus from the dead (Eph. 1:19-20).

Comfort: There was no promise that life in Christ would be without pain, but that He would comfort us, He would heal us. God's Spirit can so heal your wounds that you will be stronger and more joyful when all this is over than before the hurt came into your life.

Guidance: "What to do" is always the big concern. Guidance is given by the Holy Spirit as He reveals Jesus to us. We have simply to follow Him.

Any one of several books may be of help to you as you seek to be filled with the Holy Spirit. I recommend, *With the Holy Spirit and with Fire*, by Samuel Shoemaker, or *The Holy Spirit and You*," by Dennis and Rita Bennett.

"Now, I don't want to get into something emotional," some people respond. Are you kidding? What could be more emotional than the situation you are in right now?

I know many people who have found the strength to cope with serious family problems through receiving the Holy Spirit. One such couple watched their son reject the church in which they had reared him and start running with a wild crowd. He became heavily involved in rock music and with people they knew to be doing drugs. They saw him getting farther and farther from them and felt powerless to do anything about it.

This couple was deeply involved in the church. He led the choir and was on the official board, and she was active in women's work.

"Something was missing," he told me. "In spite of my church involvement, I was not experiencing anything I could pass on to my son."

They began attending a prayer group where people had found a new reality in the Holy Spirit. Soon they became open to the idea of being filled with the Holy Spirit. Through the ministry of that group, they were baptized in the Holy Spirit and, today, are radiantly alive by His power.

In the Holy Spirit, they found the power, the guidance, and the faith, to minister to their son and many other youngsters who needed a touch of reality.

3. *Allow the Holy Spirit to strengthen you.* Your child needs to be able to look to you for strength. You can be a tower of strength only if you allow the Spirit of God to strengthen you from within.

". . . Those who look to the Lord will win new strength," is Isaiah's promise based on his own personal experience (Isa. 40:31). God wants to build you up in His strength so that you can not only stand for yourself, but bring strength to those around you. It doesn't make any difference how weak you are now, His strength can make you as strong as a giant.

One thing that has helped me tremendously to get through difficult situations is "praying in the Spirit," or "praying in tongues." After I had been baptized in the Holy Spirit, I asked God to give me a heavenly language in which to praise Him, and He did. As I praise Him, I am built up and encouraged inside, just as Paul promised: "He who speaks in a tongue edifies himself (I Cor. 14:4 RSV). Paul spoke out against the abuse of the gift in public, but confessed, "I thank God that I speak in tongues more than you all" (I Cor. 14:18 RSV). Paul needed a lot of "edifying," or "building up," and he apparently found this edification through praying in tongues in his private devotions. Don't ask me how it works. All I know is that it is a tremendous help to me and many others in wrestling against "spiritual wickedness in high places" (Eph. 6:12 KJV).

4. *Seek the fellowship of the Body of Christ.* God recognizes that you have not only a spirit and a soul—you also have a body. Thus, He offers you the fellowship of His Body, the Church.

Find a group of people—maybe in your church, maybe outside it—who have found the stream of God's Spirit and are living in it. You'll be amazed at how many of them will help to bear your burden and give strength to you.

A friend of mine recently moved to another city and almost immediately sent back word about the body of Christians he had found there. "What a delight!" he said. "These people are so free in their worship, so alive, so loving— They've helped us tremendously."

There is a massive movement of God's Spirit among people all over the world today. Almost anywhere you go, there are groups of these "live coals" who meet regularly. Ask the Lord to guide you to the one for you.

Conclusion

The best way for you to bring life to the situation of death in which you now find yourself is to let God give you His new life. He can and will give you the power to face anything—not just with a negative kind of resignation, but with adequacy. This is not some utopian dream, it is a reality in the lives of thousands of people. If you are not experiencing it, you are living beneath your privileges and robbing those around you of the strength and life they so desperately need.

Chapter 6

Let the Love Flow

Love is not merely the absence of hate. It is the positive presence of the redemptive power of God at work. The most effective thing that you, or anyone else, can do to help a person hooked on drugs is to provide a channel through which God's love can flow.

Love bears the same relationship to hate that light bears to darkness. When you walk into a dark room, you don't reach for a bucket and start bailing out the darkness. You turn on the light and the darkness disappears. The degree of light is directly related to the power of the light source. Light dispels darkness, not vice versa. Love dispels hate, life conquers death, health conquers sickness, peace conquers strife, and order conquers chaos in God's system.

Enough of God's love poured into any life can transform that life into the beautiful thing God created it to be. Please note that I said "love" and not "words about love."

Do you want to let the love flow into your child's life? If you have taken seriously the previous chapter, then it will flow. If you are hoping to skip that chapter and produce the love on your own, the best you can hope for is a slight trickle. The following are suggestions for directing the stream of love to the point of greatest need.

Be Real

Get honest. If all you can do now is to struggle for the life-giving stream of God's Spirit, don't be afraid to reveal this to your child. Don't try to fake it! You can't pull it off. Don't talk about love by denouncing him for his lack of it; don't cover up your hypocrisy by trying to point up his; don't try to tell him about peace with God while you are frantically pacing the floor and popping tranquilizers or downing a martini. If all this makes you angry, maybe the most helpful thing you can do is take a look at why.

Think of the qualities you would most like to see in your child's life, and dedicate yourself to the task of making them a reality in your own life. You cannot push him an inch, but you can lead him as far as he needs to go.

Let me suggest some of the qualities you might let the Holy Spirit cultivate in your life. As you demonstrate these "fruits of the Spirit," listed in Galatians 5:22-23, your child's life will be affected. (This list is taken from the wording of the Phillips translation of the New Testament.)

Love—For a good definition of love, turn to I Corinthians 13.

Joy—Not happiness, mind you, but joy. Happiness is directly dependent on circumstances. Joy is the direct result of relationship with God. It is divinely imparted and cannot be crushed, no matter how bad the outward circumstances. It was joy that caused Paul and Silas to break out into song that night they were in the Philippian jail with their backs torn to shreds. Your child's search into drugs indicates that, while he has been trying to find happiness in "kicks," what he has really been looking for is real joy, which is a spiritual thing.

Peace—Not merely the absence of conflict, but the positive presence of inner tranquillity that cannot be disturbed no matter how threatening the forces of the enemy. Peace is that divinely given assurance that God is in complete command (Isa. 26:3). It comes from absolute trust.

I once went with a fifteen-year-old girl to tell her mother that she was pregnant.

"Oh God, no! He's a junkie!" the mother screamed when told who the father of the unborn child was. She was right; the boy was shooting a lot of "speed" and was selling dope to finance his habit.

"I don't think I can stand it," she went on. Some years earlier, her husband had died suddenly after they had had a violent argument. She had lived with feelings of guilt, financial insecurity, and loneliness. Adding the pain of this situation seemed overwhelming.

That night, the mother and daughter

and I sat and talked for a long time, during which I encouraged them to get all their feelings of anger and hurt out into the open. Then we prayed together. I watched as this mother and daughter joined hands and asked for God's help in coping with the problem. They both admitted that what was taking place was overpowering them, and that their only hope was in God.

I prayed that God's peace would be given, and then we just waited silently before the Lord. What took place was miraculous. Slowly all the anger and anxiety began to leave. During the next few days, we were able to talk about all the decisions that had to be made and take the necessary actions without the highly charged emotional atmosphere that had been present before. The external situation was not changed, but the people involved became able to cope with it.

Patience—The drug addict doesn't need condemnation, he needs help.

Recently, I called a father who might well have been justified in saying, "Here we go again." His son had telephoned from a distant city and told us that he was losing his long bout with hepatitis and was seriously ill. He wanted to come home.

During the previous three years, this boy had gone off to do his dope and beer many times. Whenever he got into trouble, he would come home for help, and as soon as he was on his feet, he would take off again.

I told the father that we would bring the boy home, and he assured me that he would do all that he could to help.

"Maybe he means business this time," he said hopefully.

Kindness—Give him what you would like to receive if the situation were reversed—if you were in his shoes. Give him not what you would expect, but what you would like to receive.

Generosity—This is not to suggest you let your child con you. What he needs from you is the benefit of the doubt.

Fidelity—Recently, a man in our city was faced with a situation involving his son and drugs. A friend said to him, "I know this must be embarrassing to you." I heard the father reply, "He may be terrible in the eyes of the world, and I am disappointed with his actions, but he is still my son." Can your child depend on you for this kind of faithfulness?

Tolerance—This suggests an acceptance of the person even though everything within you rejects his actions.

Self-Control—Not only does this ask that we not lose our tempers, it demands that we not come apart at the seams.

Actions may seem very important to you, but attitudes are what will make the difference. Many parents want me to tell them specifically what they should do. I have found that if the attitude is not right, there is nothing I can tell them that will work, and if the attitude is right, they don't need me, or anyone, to tell them what to do.

Inspire Hope

Drug addicts are among the most hopeless people I have ever seen. Most of their hopes are based on lies. They live in a fantasy world, and deep inside they know it is an escape from reality.

The addict's life is built on lies. He may have looked at life through distorted eyes for so long that he cannot recognize reality when he sees it. What he needs from you is the confidence that he is going to make it.

This is a delicate situation. You need to be very careful that you don't convey to him the feeling that you believe his lies or that the world is as he sees it. You certainly don't want to come across as "cocky" in saying that you know something that he doesn't. What you need to convey is the feeling that you see the situation, in all its ugliness, but that your confidence is based on the hope that God is going to intervene to help everyone involved. Let him know also that you believe in the inherent good in him.

A girl who was heavily into hallucinogenic drugs came to me for help. I suggested that we talk to her parents and ask for their help. "Oh, no!" she responded, "My mother would die if she knew how much I had tripped out— She couldn't take it!" I knew her mother and suspected she was right.

Remember the father we referred to earlier who said to his daughter, "I believe you are going to make it"? There was no hint that he was denying how bad the situation was. It was more like saying, "I know how bad the situation is, I see the worst, but my faith in God

and in you assures me that tomorrow is
going to be a better day."

Hear

I have a friend, a Spirit-filled psycho-
logical counselor, who sits in interces-
sory prayer the whole time a person is
talking to him. This is a beautiful tech-
nique, because it enables God to reveal
to him the meaning behind the words.
Sometimes, what you hear a person say
is not what he means at all. It is not
enough to listen—you have to hear.

Recently, I had an appointment with a
young man who wanted me to help a
friend of his. Yet this fellow, with his
$100-a-day cocaine habit, needed help
for himself more than anyone I knew.

As I talked with the "cocaine freak,"
I began to pray, "Lord, help me to really
hear this person, to see him as You see
him, to look beyond the story he's telling
me now and see what is really going on
inside him."

Suddenly, I saw and heard him in a
new light. By coming to me for his
friend, he was making the first steps
toward coming for himself. Scared to

trust me with his problems, he threw out those of his friend to see if I would be understanding and truly helpful.

It's important for you to try this same kind of hearing behind the words to understand your child and where he really stands.

"I hate you," sometimes means, "I'm frightened, I feel alone, I feel guilty, I'm in pain."

"Get out of my life," often means, "I'm afraid you are going to desert me. I'd rather kick you out than to have the hurt of seeing you walk away."

"Get off my back," usually means, "Things are coming at me so fast, and from so many directions, that I cannot assimilate them. I can't even bring my life under control enough to meet *my* standards—much less yours."

"Nobody understands me," quite frequently means, "I don't understand myself, or anybody else, for that matter."

"Pigs, fascists, hypocrites," is another way of saying, "I have not been able to make my relationships with people work. Since I cannot take the pain of admitting my failure, I must blame it on something."

"My friends don't hassle me," usually

indicates, "I cannot compete in your world, but with my friends, I don't have to. They're as messed up as I am."

I am not suggesting that you start trying to interpret *to him* what his words mean. But ask God to help you hear between the words. Remember, a drug addict is almost completely deceived by Satan's lies. He probably believes that he feels the way he is talking. But as you begin to understand his feelings and respond to them rather than to the alarming and offensive things he says, you'll be more at ease with him and able to let God's love flow.

Don't let his arrogant attitude annoy you either. Arrogance is almost always a defense mechanism to hold people at bay.

We once had a little dog that got caught in a drainpipe. She was frightened nearly to death. I reached in to pull her out, and she began to bite me furiously. I tried to calm her, but the more I tried to rescue her, the more she tried to chew up my hands. Finally, I went and got some thick gloves and pulled her, biting and yelping, from the pipe. Once out, her whole character changed. She began to jump and yelp joyously. I could easily have believed that she was trying to apologize for biting me. That happens very often with kids when they come out of drug addiction. They may be ever so arrogant while they are in trouble, but when it is all over, those toward whom they have been most arrogant become the objects of their greatest affection.

Pray

"If you can't do anything else, you can pray," is the usual attitude about prayer. My advice in a serious drug crisis would almost be, "If you can pray, don't do anything else."

There is no one who will intercede for your child as devotedly as you will, and there is nothing else you can do that will be as productive.

Prayer is not talking God into doing something He doesn't want to do, it is creating a climate on earth in which the love of heaven can flow freely. The process of prayer is the process of becoming one with God—uniting your heart with His for the thing you want most to happen and the thing He died to provide.

"I don't even know how to pray, what to ask for," many parents have said to me at this point. Here's where the Holy Spirit takes over. Sometimes, all you can do is to groan at the pain and confusion you feel. Paul said, "The Spirit itself maketh intercession for us with groanings which cannot be uttered" (Rom. 8:26 KJV). The value of praying in the Spirit cannot be overemphasized. There are times when all I can do is to lie on my back and cry. At such times, the Holy Spirit comes through with that heavenly language and prays for me. He reaches in and gathers up all the needs and pains and presents them to God for me in a way I never could. He tells God about needs I don't even know I have.

When the Holy Spirit presents our needs to the Father, there comes an assurance that cannot be described. It is the "peace which passes understanding."

But prayer is not all asking—it is primarily praise and thanksgiving. "Be thankful, whatever the circumstances may be" (I Thess. 5:18 Phillips).

The greatest release you will ever find will come through your learning how to

praise God in the midst of the most difficult circumstances.

"Don't worry over anything whatever; tell God every detail of your needs
in earnest and thankful prayer, and the
peace of God, which transcends human
understanding, will keep constant guard
over your hearts and minds as they rest
in Christ Jesus" (Phil. 4:6-7 Phillips).

Allow God to Work—His Way

Can you trust God to take over the
situation? Can you really believe that
"in everything . . . he [God] co-operates
for good with those who love God"?
(Rom. 8:28). The pressure is to "do
something" yourself; to try to change
the situation. But the truth is that if you
could correct the problem, you could
have prevented it.

The tendency is to turn things over to
God and then, when He starts working,
to panic. You see, God's ways are not
ours, and sometimes it appears that God
is going to kill the person rather than
heal him.

A girl came to me once, deeply troubled over someone she loved who was

heavily into dope. We talked, then prayed, and she turned it over to the Lord.
We agreed to each pray thirty minutes
each day for the young man until the
Lord brought him out. Ten days later he
was arrested.

The day he was arrested, the girl pan-
icked and went running to bail him out
of jail, breaking our agreement when
things got "worse" rather than "better."

I've seen some strange things happen
when we began praying for drug addicts.
Many are arrested, some get violently
ill, girls have gotten pregnant, some
have attempted suicide.

Things often get worse because God
has to bring a person to a point of des-
peration before He can work redemp-
tively in his life. This is painful to watch.
Yet I have never seen a drug addict
cured before he reached the point of des-
peration. Some seem to sink lower than
others, but for each there is that point at
which he says, "Things just can't go on
this way."

It is not enough for you or me to sit on
the sidelines and say that. The addict
himself has to come to that point at
which he is ready to cry out, "God, have

mercy on me, a sinner." Only then can he receive what God wants to give him.

It is foolish to ask God to bring the person to a state where he is ready to change and then to get in His way as He tries to work, yet this is what we do instinctively.

Once, when I was deeply troubled, trying to help several people who were hooked on drugs, the Lord showed me a vision. I saw a brick mason hard at work building a beautiful house. He carefully placed and leveled each brick. Soon the mason had worked his way around to the back, out of sight. A group of children were playing in the front yard, building sandcastles. "Let's help him build the house," one of them said. Pretty soon they were rearranging bricks everywhere. Then it happened—One of the children pulled out a key brick, and the whole front wall came crashing down. "But, we were only trying to help!" the child explained to the mason as he came around to investigate the noise.

The point was clear. The mason was representative of Jesus, hard at work in the lives of those I wanted to reach for Him. I was as the children, trying to help, but only undoing what Jesus was doing.

Once you have given your life and the whole family crisis to the Lord, keep your hands off. Expect Him to keep His promise; expect Him to perform whatever miracle is needed to transform everyone involved.

The Bible is filled with promises that God will meet your needs. You can count on Him to come through when everyone else around you fails. You can depend on Him, even though all the evidence points to the opposite conclusion. He's going to be there, not just because He promised, but because He cares.

Chapter 7

Care and Feeding
of a Newborn Christian

"Oh, Tom! Millie accepted the Lord last night. We had such a beautiful talk. I think we are home free now," an excited mother once told me.

"Hold on!" I said. "Not so fast. We've got a long way to go."

Accepting the Lord, being filled with the Spirit, and being delivered are just first steps toward establishing a vital, mature relationship with God. A lot of nurture is required for spiritual growth. Without it, a young Christian is going to fall right back into the old way. If that happens, you have a bigger mess than ever on your hands.

In this chapter, we shall take a look at

what is going on now, what is likely to emerge, and your role in the Christian growth process.

"I've Got a Fanatic on My Hands"

"I'd rather she be on drugs than to be the way she is now," a deeply disturbed father told me. "She's become a religious fanatic."

"What do you mean?" I asked.

"All she wants to talk about is Jesus. She talks to everybody about God and tries to convert everyone she meets," he said. "Last night she tried to convert my boss. She was downright offensive."

"Praise the Lord!" I said.

What was happening to this girl was as natural as eating when she was hungry. Her newfound freedom was like that of a bird just let out of a cage. She had to try her wings. Also, her faith was so new that it was still hard for her to trust it. The only way to make sure it would not go away was to talk to everybody about it.

"Emotionalism" bothers a lot of adults, but teenagers are emotional creatures. When all of the feelings of guilt, fear, and loneliness are suddenly and dramatically replaced by the love and power of God, something has to give. Usually, when a life that has been filled with hate is suddenly filled with love, the person standing closest by is going to get his neck hugged.

"Why can't she just settle down and become a nice girl like Rhonda?" the father asked.

"Because she is herself, her wonderful, redeemed self," I replied.

One thing that excites me so much about the so-called Jesus Movement is the excitement with which new converts begin the new life in Christ. There is something beautiful about the way God bursts forth with new joy on the youthful enthusiasm. Staid old churchmen often set themselves to the task of settling down these new "fanatics." But it is far better to channel that spiritual energy than to try to crush it.

The most wonderful thing in the world has happened to that new child of God. Why shouldn't he be excited?

Relax! What God has started, He can finish. That burst of radiance is the expression of a personal experience your child has had with God. It is his, and that makes it valid.

"The Bottom Fell Out"

"Tom, I feel awful. It's gone. I feel more mixed up than I did before I became a Christian," the girl described above said to me a week later.

"See, I told you it wouldn't last," her father was quick to point out.

What usually happens in the early stages of spiritual growth is a burst of strong feeling that lasts for a short period of time, and then the bottom falls out. We call it "growing pains."

The Lord gives that tremendous burst of feeling at the beginning because He knows we need a glimpse of what it is like to live in complete union with Him. But He knows that, as a steady diet, such euphoria would make us spiritual weaklings and spoiled brats. So He moves us on to stronger food as soon as He thinks we are ready. There is no such thing as a static relationship with God. We are either growing up or shriveling up.

When the bottom falls out, a person

needs encouragement to keep on going. He needs more prayer and understanding than ever. He has a lot of things to work out in his new relationship with God. These things take time and often come at the cost of great pain and frustration.

About the only fruits of the Spirit that a new Christian can produce are joy and a kind of "spiritual puppy love." He certainly hasn't developed a Christ-like spirit overnight. But don't get down on him or disappointed in God.

At first, we see the face of Jesus at a distance. It is so beautiful that we know we must see it at closer range. When we see the terrain we must cross to get nearer to Him, it is pretty frightening.

What You Can Do to Help

1. *Provide leadership and strength.* You can do a lot to help with the process of growth toward spiritual and emotional maturity, if you remember that your youngster needs to develop at his own pace and in his own way.

If your child has responded to Christ, what has happened is completely miraculous, and if he is to grow up in the Lord, it will be through continued divine intervention.

Lead—don't push. Be available—don't crowd. A judgmental attitude that says, "Good Christians don't do that," is not nearly so helpful as one that accepts and asks, "How do you feel about that?"

Look to the future. Someone has said that because of the cross of Christ, "There is no past in the future and no future in the past." Often the emphasis on what a person has come out of makes his Christian commitment focus on rebellion against drugs. Such a stance is not much of a vantage point from which to launch a glorious future. Seek to lead the convert into the newness of life which is offered by God, and admonish him to forget the past.

There is always something new to learn and experience in the Lord. As you discover new truths in God, invite your child to share in that growth experience. Again, seek to make it exciting for him rather than trying to force the issue.

Teenagers have seemingly boundless energy, and this is certainly true of a converted "drug freak." One of the big things a newly delivered drug addict has to contend with is time on his hands.

Probably the process of getting dope, doing dope, and covering up for it has consumed hours and hours of his time in the past. Now that he doesn't have that kind of activity, he may get bored pretty easily. Try to channel that energy into some constructive action, not by telling him what he ought to be doing, but by offering enough opportunities that some of them appear attractive to him.

2. *Provide reading materials and growth experiences*. There are many publications available to encourage Christian growth.

A visit to a Christian bookstore or the book table at a Christian growth conference can be a good investment of time and money.

Whenever you make available materials you have read, offer to discuss the truths you discovered and be interested in the youngster's reaction. Frank, open conversation can be most helpful in cementing a new relationship. Besides, you might learn something useful yourself.

Music is another important factor in communicating with youths. I would strongly suggest that you help your child find music to which he can relate. Often teenagers are forced to listen to the pop music stations, with all their emphasis on dope, sex, and rebellion, because they cannot find a musical expression that is both Christian and exciting. You don't have to like or understand contemporary Christian music to see that it has value if it communicates God's love to those who do like and understand it.

Several radio shows are now making a lot of impact on Christian youths. To find out if one of those shows is broadcast on a station in your area you might try writing to "The Scott Ross Show," Freeville, New York, "Songtime," in Boston, Mass., or to "The Lovelight Salvation Show," P. O. Box 485, High Point, N.C. You might also ask radio stations in your area for a program schedule. Look for shows with youth appeal.

Retreats, camps, and special growth conferences are being held all over the United States now, and many of these provide excellent opportunities for learning more about "life in the Spirit." These are often publicized through Christian bookstores and such monthly magazines as *Logos Journal*, *New Wine Magazine*, and *Voice*. If you cannot find suitable conferences in your area, write

Youth Unlimited, Inc., P.O. Box 485, High Point, North Carolina 27261, and we will try to help you locate a source of information.

3. *Maintain your own spiritual growth.* Perhaps the most important thing you can do is to maintain open channels of communication with God yourself. You cannot lead your child into experiences with God that are not a real part of your own personal experience. Stay in fellowship with other Christians who are earnestly seeking to learn more about Christ. A list of books I have found helpful is included at the end of this book.

Your own experience of growing with God will have a great impact on the life of your family. It can also help to prevent problems of the past from recurring.

4. *Trust God and your child.* Many parents feel that they can take over after God has bailed them out of a bad situation. Don't try it. If God has begun a work, trust Him to complete what He has started. You may not understand some of the things that begin to happen, but it is important that you trust God to see the problem all the way through.

It is also important to trust your child

in his Christian growth. Give him the freedom to worship God in a way that meets his own needs.

Talk openly with him about the things he is learning and experiencing. Some of the things he says may not set so well with your theology, but trust the Holy Spirit to guide him into the Truth that Jesus promised. Don't worry so much about doctrinal points on which you disagree. God will show him if he is wrong.

Many parents get disturbed over the fact that their child would rather worship with a bunch of "Jesus freaks" than attend church services with the family. Remember, this is *his* relationship with God, and he must develop it in his own way. Many youths have not found a satisfying worship experience in the traditional church. That may come in time, but for now, it is more important that he worship than that he worship in a way that you approve.

If he is attending worship and Bible study regularly, encourage him to do so. You might even drop a hint that you would like to go with him. If he invites you, take him up on it.

Chapter 8

Some Practical Considerations

While the presence of a delinquent child upsets practically everything in the life of the family, the business of running a home must be kept going. Decisions, often serious ones, must be made by parents, and rarely is there time to consider all the consequences or alternatives—if there are any.

In this final chapter, we want to offer some guidelines for dealing with the crises in the context of family life. The following suggestions have grown out of experiences with many families. Again, they are not "Watson's Law." You must weigh the guidelines and decide for yourself.

WHAT CAN I DO?

Should I go after my runaway child?
Generally, a person fifteen or under
should be pursued with the full assis-
tance of the police. However, the less
publicity, the better. Don't expect much
help from the child's friends. One of the
cardinal rules of the drug culture is,
"Don't rat on anybody."

The closer a child is to his sixteenth
birthday, the more fruitless will be your
search—even if you find the youngster.
If a sixteen-year-old has run away,
whether you like it or not, he is beginning to make decisions for himself. If he
doesn't want to be found, your chances
of finding him are slim.

In any case, on the trip home from the
first junket, the young person over juvenile age* should be told that next time
you won't come looking for him. Otherwise, the running away might become a
regular exercise.

What about the other children? What
to tell the other children about the absence of a teenager is often a real dilem-

*The legal age for juvenile classification
varies from state to state. You can find
out what it is in your state with a phone
call to the local police department.

ma. Small children cannot comprehend the scope of the situation, so a simple "He's gone with some friends" is usually sufficient.

However, an attempt to cover up for a runaway teenager can backfire. I have seen many such situations, but one stands out as particularly painful.

A girl I'll call Karen had left home with friends after an emotionally charged encounter with her parents. The younger sister was told that Karen had gone to visit a relative. The next day at school, Karen's friends told the younger sister about Karen's running away, and she became very upset. She called her friends liars and defended her sister. Later, when the truth came out, she was hurt and embarrassed; the damage had been done.

By the time a youngster is ten years old, it is going to be pretty difficult to pull off a lie. When he learns the truth, he is going to feel left out of the family and is likely to resent what he may interpret as lack of trust of him. Sometimes, you'd be surprised at what he already knows.

In general, the best policy is openness about the general situation, leaving out unnecessary details and speculations. There is nothing to be gained by sacrificing your relationship with one child for that with another with whom your relationship is already on shaky ground.

What do I say to him when he comes home? What to say to the runaway when he comes home has to be your decision, prayerfully arrived at, and it has to be based on the needs of the individual concerned. Here are some suggestions of things you might cover:

—Assure him that you are glad he is home and that he is safe.
—Let him know that the home is his to enjoy but not to run.
—Tell him you are available to talk about the problem in the relationship, but that you are not going to try to pound it out of him.
—Make it clear that privileges of the home—car, allowance, etc.—will be granted in direct proportion to his assumption of responsibility.
—Allow him to help you formulate some rules for his behavior. Once you have come up with a set of privileges and responsibilities, hold his feet to the fire.

—Offer outside help, but don't force it, unless he is clearly psychotic.

—Offer help in dealing with the problem of getting back in school, but don't try to suffer his consequences for him.

I strongly recommend that a neutral party preside at the first meeting between parents and a returned runaway. Often things are said in haste and in the strain of emotions that are very hard to overcome later.

Usually there are two parents against one child. Because of this authority structure, a youngster quite often feels defensive, and his fear of being crushed comes out as anger. Since your purpose is to restore the relationship, anything that can be done to eliminate defensiveness will be helpful.

However, you should be cautious that you do not give the impression of further "ganging up on" the runaway. He should be consulted as to whom you are going to ask to sit in on the session. Some suggested persons are ministers, Family Service Bureau counselors, and concerned teachers.

Often a child feels his only recourse in

dealing with a "stacked" confrontation is to run away again. With a neutral person present, you can afford to be firm without being overpowering.

Parents often take the action of a runaway as an indication of failure on their part. It is not so important to "fix the blame" on anyone as it is to admit that the relationship has not worked, and something needs to be done.

Approach that initial encounter with hope, and talk as much as possible in the future tense.

What about the use of a car? The use of the family car, or his own personal vehicle, is often a bone of real contention. As a privilege, it can often be used as a strong tool to get a teenager to assume responsibilities.

One point that must be considered is the matter of legality. In most states, an automobile used to transport drugs can be confiscated by the state and sold at public auction to defray the cost of fines, court costs, and jail fees. It should be made clear that any evidence of transporting of drugs will be sufficient to bar the child from future use of the vehicle.

Also, the driving of a vehicle by a person under the influence of drugs raises some serious moral questions. If your child chooses not to exercise good judgment, you have to assume the responsibility to see that he does not use the vehicle in a manner that may make it a weapon killing an innocent victim.

Should I bail him out of jail? As tough as it may be on you, leaving a young person in jail for a few days is often a great deal of help to him. It may save him from time in prison later. Whether you use time in jail in this way or post bail depends on the seriousness of the charge and the age of the person involved.

He will usually protest his innocence and demand release. While he may not be guilty of the specific charge against him, or while the arrest may not have been entirely within his constitutional protection, I would caution you against allowing him to think that you will take up his cause against the police. During the last five years, I have seen many trumped-up cases, but I have never seen a youngster arrested on a drug charge who was not in some way involved in drug traffic.

In any event, the teenager should be made to assume the cost of arranging his own bail bond.

It is very important that you don't bear the costs of his drug activities. If there are fines, fees, or any other costs incurred from his illegal activities, they lose all their deterrent value when you "take his rap." Besides, other members of the family have to be considered.

I know a woman who is hopelessly in debt because of money she has paid out on legal fees, while her son is on the west coast, living it up. Another family spent so much on one child's drug involvement that other children have been deprived of educational opportunities. If your child gets the idea that you will "pay him out of trouble," you are in for a merry ride.

Should I get him an attorney? On a first offense, an attorney should be employed. However, it should be done only after the teenager agrees to earn the money to pay the fee. If possible, the fee should be handled between the teenager and the attorney.

One caution about attorneys. Often, there are one or two "hot shot" lawyers in a town who are noted for "getting people off on any charge." While getting your child off might seem to solve the immediate problem, it often gives him the feeling that he cannot be stopped. A probation period is usually more desirable than dropping the charges.

And, don't forget, there's more to a trial than what goes on between judge and lawyer. The attitude of the child and his parents will have far more influence on the judge than the maneuverings of a sharp lawyer.

Once you have obtained a lawyer, follow his advice in all matters unless what he advises violates your Christian conscience.

Should I attend the trial? If it is possible, both parents should attend the trial. There is nothing that makes a person feel less loved than to be deserted by his parents in his greatest hour of need. And there is nothing that infuriates a judge more than to see a kid come to trial without his parents.

Should I try to get him some literature while he's in jail? Try to get someone else—a minister, friend, or a Christian attorney—to take your child some good Christian reading material while he is in jail. This is better than taking it to him yourself.

Some good books are:

Love Can Open Prison Doors, by Starr Daily.

The Cross and the Switchblade, by David Wilkerson.

Run, Baby, Run, by Nicky Cruz.

Good News for Modern Man, a modern translation of the New Testament.

Your child may resent the literature at first, but in the dragging hours, he may start reading it with good results.

What if he goes to prison? If your child is sentenced to prison, all you can do is write him regularly, visit him when permitted, and pray without ceasing.

Help him wait out the sentence. It may be that God will work that miracle behind cell walls that He could not do while your child was free to run his merry way.

Many states are experimenting with

release programs which will allow family members to pick up a person from prison and take him out for a few hours, or for a weekend. These can be very helpful in establishing good relationships. Such visits should be under careful supervision.

Health Problems. There are many health hazards involved in drug abuse. One of the most common is hepatitis. It often starts with one person and is transferred via a dirty needle or orally to other members of a drug ring. Should you suspect hepatitis, try to get the infected person to a doctor for a check-up. Once hepatitis is confirmed, or even strongly suspected, all persons living with the carrier should be inoculated for their protection. This disease is highly contagious and can be quite serious.

Venereal diseases are another set of problems within the drug culture. You had better face the ugly fact that if your youngster is heavily involved in drugs, he is probably involved in illicit sex activity. I don't think I have ever met a person who was heavily into dope who was not also involved in sexual activities. Unfortunately, if your child picks up a venereal disease, you will probably be the last person to know about it. Doctors and health clinics will treat the sufferer from VD without notifying parents or authorities. No criminal prosecution is involved, but a person treated will be asked about his sexual contacts in an effort to slow down the spread of the disease. An effort will be made by the medical team to find and treat others who may be infected.

What should I do if my daughter turns up pregnant? Premarital pregnancy is a distressing fact of life for a great number of teenage girls. Should you find out your daughter is pregnant, particularly if she comes to you, assure her of your love and offer your help.

First, get her to a doctor to confirm the pregnancy and its timing. Talk openly with the doctor about all of the options open to her. He can help in any direction she chooses to go.

I can't stress too heavily the importance of the involvement of a doctor in all negotiations. Most of the medical studies I have read indicate that a child whose parents have been involved in drugs is more likely to be born with birth defects than one whose parents have not used drugs.

Should a girl decide to abort the child, there is little you can do to stop her. I've seen girls do all kinds of things from taking a pill calculated to make them abort to going to a clandestine operator who will do the job for them in the back room. Back-room abortions have a notoriously high mortality rate. Open, loving communication on this subject is absolutely vital.

Where can I get information on specific drugs? A great deal of information about drugs has been published in the last few years, much of it misleading, doing more harm than good. The most reliable source I have found for drug publications is the National Institute of Mental Health, Bethesda, Maryland.

One caution: don't try to become an expert. Drug "lingo" varies widely from time to time and from one locale to another. It is not really important to be able to talk intelligently about drugs. Stick to your own areas of competence and be yourself. It is much better to be real than to try to be "hip."

WHAT CAN I DO?

What if my child won't talk to me?
Don't try to force it. When pressure is
applied before a person is ready to talk,
he is invariably forced into dishonesty.
Dishonest communication is worse than
no communication at all.

Be ready to listen, but be aware that
you cannot force the issue with good results.

Many times a parent will become angry because his child talks quite openly
to a minister, or Sunday school teacher,
or someone else, while remaining silent
with him. The parent who can communi-
cate with a child while he is going
through a drug experience is an extreme
rarity. If the child will talk with anyone
outside his circle of destructive friends,
you are ahead of the game. Most kids
open up to someone else before they
open up to their parents, and this kind of
communication should be encouraged.

*How does the occult fit into the drug
picture?* Several major universities are
researching the connection of hallucinogenic drugs with "supernatural" phe-
nomena. Through their parapsychology
departments, they are looking into drug-

related extrasensory perception, clairvoyance, and a host of unusual claims of the drug culture and are finding some surprising facts. Not much of a really dependable nature has yet been published of their findings on the subject.

Most adults tend to be pretty naïve about occult practices that are going on commonly throughout the country. Ouija boards, horoscopes, "Satan music"—these may seem harmless enough on the surface, but I have talked with many kids who have gotten into them over their heads. Whether you take it seriously or not, many of them do.

Evidences of the occult are everywhere. One of the biggest and most consistently popular songs in the rock music scene is "Sympathy for the Devil," by a group called "The Rolling Stones." Records have been sold by the thousands during the last few years with such names as "Witch-Coven" and "Satanic Mass." There are groups of witches meeting in almost every state of the union.

Most youngsters who get involved with the occult blunder into it rather than searching for it. A boy recently told me of going to a commune after running away from home.

"The people seemed all right to me. They did a lot of dope, but that was what I wanted," he said. "I was from a Pentecostal family, and I was surprised that some of the people in the commune spoke in tongues and talked constantly about prophecies."

He began to notice that something was amiss when he wasn't allowed into the worship services of the commune. As the days wore on, he became attracted to the high priestess of the commune, and they began taking long walks together. Gradually, he learned that she was a priestess of Satan and that the commune was centered in Satan worship.

Finally, the "priestess" went into "meditation" for several days and, when she returned, announced that Satan had told her to marry the young man.

"That was too much for me," he said. That night he slipped out of a window and fled through the snow. When I talked with him months later, he told me of almost continuous "spiritual hassling" since that time.

Some youths do not get out that easily.

Escape from Witchcraft, by Roberta Blankenship and *The Satan-Seller*, by Mike Warnke are the best personal-encounter volumes I have seen.

For further information, I would suggest *The Back Side of Satan*, by Morris Cerullo, and *The Challenging Counterfeit*, by Raphael Gasson.

I would caution against confronting a youngster with your fear that he may be involved in the occult unless you are especially anointed by the Holy Spirit to do so. Some things you might look for are participation in hypnosis, use of the Ouija board, and preoccupation with horoscopes. It is also a very good idea to know who is chaperoning those "pajama parties." If you find some evidence your child is involved in occultism, seek help from people who really know how to pray.

The best defense against spiritual forces is an active prayer life—preferably with a prayer group.

What should I do if I suspect my child is using dope? Don't panic! An over-emotional response from you is sure to make the situation worse.

"Should I confront my child with what

I have found?" is a question I am commonly asked. Of course, you cannot simply ignore concrete evidence of drug usage, but I have never seen a parent win in the "slug fest" that is sure to follow an accusation of drug activity.

If your child has become careless enough to leave incriminating things around for you to find, you can be pretty sure that he has been doing dope a fairly long time. He may even be hoping that you will find dope in his room so that his feelings of guilt can be covered up by the anger and rejection he feels when you "go through the ceiling." Or, he may be subtly asking for your help. Don't blow it by trying to scream away the problem.

I would suggest the following format for dealing with the immediate crisis. If all the things I offer are not possible, use some ingenuity and come up with some alternatives.

1. Set up a meeting with the youngster for two or three days later. Simply tell him that you are concerned about some problems you see in your relationship and that you want to talk about those problems. Never hit him with your evidence when he is planning to go somewhere or in the presence of a

114

friend. You will force him to decide between you and his friends, and if he is into dope, the choice will almost always be in their favor.

2. Offer to have a mutual friend present and negotiate with him as to who that friend will be.

3. In the interim period, try to maintain as calm and normal a situation within the family as possible. Talk to a counselor yourself.

4. Never try to get some counselor to sneak up on a youngster and just casually broach the subject. Many parents have asked me to do this, and I always decline. If I have to start my work with a drug user on the basis of dishonesty, our relationship is doomed before it is begun.

5. Several things should be sought out of such a meeting:

    a. An honest discussion of the problem as you see it and as he sees it. Openness and love are the key. Don't force him into lying by an insistence on his telling the whole truth.

    b. An awareness on his part that, while you reject his behavior, you accept him as a person.

   c. A plan to deal with the problems in the relationship.

   d. A feeling of confidence that, working together, the problems in the relationship can be overcome. Remember, it is quite likely that he will not see his drug usage as a problem, but only the fact that you are uptight about it. It is important to speak in terms of the family's relationship problem and not so much about his misbehavior.

   e. Setting of limits and goals.

6. Follow through faithfully on what has been decided by the family conference.

7. Take seriously the contents of this book as a whole.

8. Pray! Pray! Pray!

I, and the people of our fellowship, will be praying that the God of miracles will work powerfully in you and your family to bring about His purposes. If we may be of help, please write to us.

As you pray, remember us.

The ministry of Youth Unlimited, Inc., is dependent on private donations, and contributions are gratefully accepted.

Checks should be made payable to Youth Unlimited, Inc., and mailed to P. O. Box 485, High Point, North Carolina 27261. Contributions are tax-deductible.

Suggested Additional Reading

The Holy Spirit and You, by Dennis and Rita Bennett. Plainfield, N.J.: Logos International, 1971.

Nine O'Clock in the Morning, by Dennis J. Bennett. Plainfield, N.J.: Logos International, 1970.

Escape from Witchcraft, by Roberta Blankenship. Grand Rapids, Mich.: Zondervan, 1972.

The Back Side of Satan, by Morris Cerullo. Carol Stream, Ill.: Creation House, 1973.

Love Can Open Prison Doors, by Starr Daily. Evesham, Worcs., England: Arthur James Ltd.

The Challenging Counterfeit, by Raphael Gasson. Plainfield, N.J.: Logos International, 1966.

With the Holy Spirit and with Fire, by Samuel M. Shoemaker. Waco, Texas: Word Books, 1970.

The Satan Seller, by Mike Warnke. Plainfield, N.J.: Logos International, 1972.

The Cross and the Switchblade, by David Wilkerson. Westwood, N.J.: Fleming H. Revell, 1963.

SUGGESTED INEXPENSIVE PAPERBACK BOOKS
. . . WHEREVER PAPERBACKS ARE SOLD
OR USE HANDY ORDER FORM.

QUANTITY			
____	AGLOW WITH THE SPIRIT—Frost	L326	.95
____	AMAZING SAINTS—Saint	L409	2.50
____	AND FORBID NOT TO SPEAK—Ervin	L329	.95
____	AND SIGNS FOLLOWED—Price	P002	1.50
____	ANGLES OF LIGHT?—Freeman	A506	.95
____	ANSWERS TO PRAISE—Carothers	L670	1.95
____	ANVIL—Orsini	P089	1.25
____	ARMSTRONG ERROR—DeLoach	L317	.95
____	AS AT THE BEGINNING—Harper	L721	.95
____	BAPTISM IN THE SPIRIT—Schep	L343	1.50
____	BAPTISM IN THE SPIRIT—BIBLICAL —Cockburn	16F	.65
____	BAPTISM OF FIRE—Harper	8F	.60
____	BAPTIZED IN ONE SPIRIT—Baker	1F	.60
____	BAPTIZED IN THE SPIRIT—Clark	P9	.75
____	BEN ISRAEL—Katz	A309	.95
____	BLACK TRACKS—Miles	A298	.95
____	BLESS YOUR DIRTY HEART—Lindsey	P017	1.95
____	BORN TO BURN—Wallace	A508	.95
____	CATHOLIC PENTECOSTALISM—McDonnell	P6	.60
____	CHALLENGING COUNTERFEIT—Gasson	L102	.95
____	CLAP YOUR HANDS—Tomczak	P073	2.50
____	COMING ALIVE—Buckingham	A501	.95
____	CONCISE GOSPELS AND ACTS —Christianson	P008	2.50
____	CONFESSIONS OF A HERETIC—Hunt	L31X	2.50
____	COUNSELOR TO COUNSELOR—Campbell	L335	1.50
____	DAYSPRING—White	L334	1.95
____	DAY THE DOLLAR DIES—Cantelon	P013	2.50
____	DISCOVERY (Booklet)—Frost	F71X	.50
____	DIVINE HEALING—Murray	P080	1.25
____	DO YOURSELF A FAVOR—Williams	P055	2.50
____	ERA OF THE SPIRIT—Williams	L322	1.95
____	FIFTEEN STEPS OUT—Mumford	L106	1.50
____	FROM THE BELLY OF THE WHALE—White	A318	.95
____	FULL BLESSING OF PENTECOST—Murray	P061	1.25
____	GATHERED FOR POWER—Pulkingham	MB1X	2.50
____	GIFT IS ALREADY YOURS—Prange	P037	2.50

PRICE SUBJECT TO CHANGE WITHOUT NOTICE

QUANTITY

GLAD YOU ASKED THAT—R. Bennett	P084	2.50
GOD BREAKS IN—Congdon	L313	1.95
GOD DID NOT ORDAIN SILENCE —Christianson	P054	2.50
GOD IS FOR THE EMOTIONALLY ILL —Guldseth	A507	.95
GOD'S JUNKIE—Arguinzoni	A509	.95
GOD'S LIVING ROOM—Walker	A123	.95
GONE IS SHADOWS' CHILD—Foy	L337	.95
GRACE AND THE GLORY OF GOD —Benson/Jarman	L104	1.50
HEALING ADVENTURE—White	L345	1.95
HEALING LIGHT—Sanford	L726	.95
HEAR MY CONFESSION—Orsini	L341	1.00
HEY GOD!—Foglio	P007	1.95
HOLY LAND HYMNS—Brumback	P087	1.45
HOLY SPIRIT AND YOU—Bennett	L324	2.50
IN THE SECRET PLACE—Van Woerdan	P081	1.25
IRELAND'S HOPE—Streeter	P027	1.25
JESUS AND ISRAEL—Benson	A514	.95
JESUS CHRIST UNIVERSITY—Summers	P051	.95
JESUS PEOPLE ARE COMING—King	A519	.95
KINGDOM OF DARKNESS—Thomas	P034	1.95
KINGDOM OF SELF—Jabay	P062	2.50
LAYMAN'S COMMENTARY HOLY SPIRIT—Rea	P014	2.50
LET THIS CHURCH DIE—Weaver	A520	.95
LET US PRAISE—Cornwall	P039	2.50
LEWI PETHRUS: SPIRITUAL MEMOIR —Pethrus	P043	1.95
LIFE IN THE HOLY SPIRIT—Harper	5F	.50
LIVING PROMISES—Summers	P986	1.25
LONELY NOW—Cruz	A510	1.25
LORD OF THE VALLEYS—Bulle	L018	2.50
LOST SHEPHERD—Sanford	L328	.95
MADE ALIVE—Price	P001	1.50
MANIFEST VICTORY—Moseley	L724	2.50
MANNERS AND CUSTOMS OF BIBLE —Freeman	P022	2.95
MICHAEL, MICHAEL—Esses	P047	2.50
MIRACLES THROUGH PRAYER—Harrell	A518	.95
MY KID'S ON DRUGS—Watson	P067	1.25
NEW TESTAMENT CHURCH BOOK—West	P045	1.95
NEW WAY OF LIVING—Harper	P066	2.50

PRICE SUBJECT TO CHANGE WITHOUT NOTICE

_____	NICKY CRUZ GIVES THE FACTS ON DRUGS —Cruz	B70	.50
_____	NINE O'CLOCK IN THE MORNING—Bennett	P555	2.50
_____	NOAH'S ARK—I TOUCHED IT—Navarra	P065	2.95
_____	NONE CAN GUESS—Harper	L722	1.95
_____	OUT OF THIS WORLD—Fisher	A517	.95
_____	OVERFLOWING LIFE—Frost	P050	2.50
_____	PASTOR'S WIFE—Wurmbrand	P032	2.50
_____	PATHWAY TO POWER—Davison	L00X	1.50
_____	PENTECOST BEHIND IRON CURTAIN —Durasoff	P018	1.50
_____	PENTECOST IN THE CATHOLIC CHURCH —O'Connor	P8	.60
_____	PENTECOSTAL REALITY—Williams	P016	1.50
_____	PENTECOSTALS—Nichol	L711	2.50
_____	PHENOMENON OF OBEDIENCE—Esses	P085	2.50
_____	PIONEERS OF REVIVAL—Clarke	L723	.95
_____	POWER IN PRAISE—Carothers	L342	1.95
_____	POWER FOR THE BODY—Harper	4F	.85
_____	PRAISE WORKS!—Carothers	P060	1.95
_____	PRAYER MEETINGS—Cavnar	P2	.50
_____	PREACHER WITH A BILLY CLUB—Asmuth	A209	.95
_____	PRISON TO PRAISE—Carothers	A504	1.25
_____	PROPHECY: A GIFT FOR THE BODY—Harper	2FXX	.65
_____	PSEUDO CHRISTIANS—Jarman	A516	.95
_____	REAL FAITH—Price	P000	1.50
_____	REMARKABLE MIRACLES—Bevington	P063	2.50
_____	RISE TO NEWNESS OF LIFE—Beal	EP01	2.95
_____	RUN BABY RUN—Cruz	L101	.95
_____	RUN BABY RUN—Cruz (ComicBook)		.25
_____	SATAN SELLER—Warnke	L794	2.50
_____	SEEDS OF CONFLICT—DeLoach	P077	2.50
_____	SET MY SPIRIT FREE—Frost	P058	2.50
_____	SOUL PATROL—Bartlett	A500	.95
_____	SPEAKING WITH GOD—Cantelon	L336	.95
_____	SPIRIT BADE ME GO—duPlessis	L325	.95
_____	SPIRITUAL AND PHYSICAL HEALTH—Price	P003	1.95
_____	SPIRITUAL GIFTS—Clark	P3	.50
_____	SPIRITUAL WARFARE—Harper	A505	.95
_____	STRONGER THAN PRISON WALLS—Wurmbrand	A956	.95
_____	SUPERNATURAL DREAMS AND VISIONS	L304	2.95
_____	TAKE ANOTHER LOOK—Mumford	L338	2.50
_____	THERE'S MORE—Hall	L344	1.50
_____	THESE ARE NOT DRUNKEN—Ervin	L105	2.50

PRICE SUBJECT TO CHANGE WITHOUT NOTICE

QUANTITY

____	THEY LEFT THEIR NETS—Pulkingham	PM02	2.50
____	THIS EARTH'S END—Benson	A513	.95
____	THIS WHICH YE SEE AND HEAR—Ervin	L728	1.95
____	TONGUES UNDER FIRE—Lillie	3F	.85
____	TURN YOUR BACK ON THE PROBLEM—Smith	L034	1.95
____	TWO WORLDS—Price	P004	1.95
____	UNDERGROUND SAINTS—Wurmbrand	U1	.95
____	WALK IN THE SPIRIT—Harper	L319	.95
____	WE'VE BEEN ROBBED—Meloon	L339	1.50
____	WHAT WILL SIMON SAY—McGinnis	P075	2.50
____	YOU CAN KNOW GOD—Price	P005	.75
____	YOUNG LIONS OF JUDAH—Evans	P059	1.25
____	YOUR NEW LOOK—Buckingham	A503	.95
____	YOUTH WITH A MISSION—Wilson	A152	.95
____	TOTAL		____

Books listed above are available wherever religious paperbacks are sold
—or order directly from:

Wholesale Book Sales
Box 292
Watchung, N.J. 07061

━━━━━━━━━ ORDER FORM ━━━━━━━━━

Please send Inspirational Books checked above—Cash, Check or
Money order must be enclosed—books will be shipped free.

TOTAL OF BOOKS ORDERED _____

TOTAL AMOUNT DUE _____
(Books shipped free)

NAME _____

STREET _____

CITY _____ STATE _____ ZIP _____

PRICE SUBJECT TO CHANGE WITHOUT NOTICE

Now you can hear famous authors . . . recorded live . . .
telling of a personal experience or testimony

CASSETTES

____	ARGUINZONI, SONNY—God's Junkie	TA17	3.95
____	BARTLETT, BOB—The Soul Patrol	TA6X	3.95
____	BENNETT, DENNIS—Nine O'Clock in The Morning	TA5X	3.95
____	BJORNSTADT, JAMES—20th Century Prophecy	JB1X	3.95
____	BREDESEN, ROBERTS—Charismatic Renewal	TA22	3.95
____	BUCKINGHAM, JAMIE—Some Gall	TA3X	3.95
____	CANTELON, WILLARD—Day The Dollar Dies	TA21	3.95
____	CAROTHERS, MERLIN—Prison to Praise	TA2X	3.95
____	CHRISTIANSON, CHRIS—God Did Not Ordain Silence	TA37	3.95
____	CORNWALL, JUDSON—Let Us Praise	TA31	3.95
____	CRUZ, NICKY—Run Baby Run	TA1X	3.95
____	duPLESSIS, DAVID—The Spirit Bade Me Go	TA11	3.95
____	DURASOFF, STEVE—Pent. Behind Iron Curtain	TA30	3.95
____	ERVIN, HOWARD—These Are Not Drunken	TA13	3.95
____	ESSES, MIKE—Michael, Michael	TA29	3.95
____	FOGLIO, FRANK—Hey God!	TA27	3.95
____	FREEMAN, HOBART—Angels of Light?	TA10	3.95
____	FROST, ROBERT—Aglow With The Spirit	TA15	3.95
____	HARPER, MICHAEL—Walk in The Spirit	TA8X	3.95
____	JARMAN, Ray—Pseudo Christians	TA7X	3.95
____	KATZ, ARTHUR—Ben Israel	TA4X	3.95
____	KUHLMAN, KATHRYN—Hour with Kuhlman	TA18	3.95
____	MUMFORD, BOB—15 Steps Out	TA9X	3.95
____	ORSINI, FR. JOSEPH—Hear My Confession	TA23	3.95
____	PRANGE, ERVIN—The Gift Is Already Yours	TA33	3.95
____	RANAGAHAN, KEVIN—Catholic Pentecostals	TA19	3.95
____	ROBERTSON, PAT—Shout It from the Housetop	TA25	3.95
____	SAINT, PHIL—Amazing Saints	TA24	3.95
____	SANFORD, AGNES—Sealed Orders	TA35	3.95
____	SIMPSON, CHARLES—So. Bapt. Looks At Pentecost	TA20	3.95
____	SMITH, MALCOLM—Turn Your Back on the Prob.	TA26	3.95
____	STREETER, PHIL—Ireland's Hope	TA32	3.95

PRICE SUBJECT TO CHANGE WITHOUT NOTICE

___	**TOMCZAK, LARRY**—Clap Your Hands	TA36	3.95
___	**WALLACE, WENDELL**—Born to Burn	TA12	3.95
___	**WARNKE, MIKE**—The Satan Seller	TA28	3.95
___	**WHITE, CLINTON**—From the Belly of the Whale	TA14	3.95
___	**WILLIAMS, J. RODMAN**—Era of the Spirit	TA16	3.95
___	**NEW TESTAMENT**—Steven B. Stevens	NTCL	69.95
	(FIFTEEN TAPES)		

___   TOTAL   ___

order from your local bookstore or

> Wholesale Book Sales
> Box 292
> Watchung, N.J. 07061

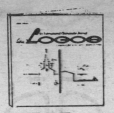

FREE
SAMPLE COPY
OF
LOGOS

An International Magazine of New Testament Christianity

Worldwide coverage of Religious News
Book Reviews
Trends and Current Issues
Feature Articles by such Internationally
known writers as:

James Lee Beal
Dennis Bennett
Harold Bredesen
Jamie
 Buckingham
Larry Christenson
Nicky Cruz
David duPlessis
Betty Lee Esses
Frank Foglio
Dr. Robert Frost
Michael Harper

Irene Burk
 Harrell
Arthur Katz
Kathryn Kuhlman
Mrs. Gordon
 Lindsay
Dan Malachuk
Peter Marshall
Bob Mumford
Father Joseph
 Orsini
Derek Prince

Pat Robertson
Agnes Sanford
Malcolm Smith
Cardinal Suenens
Corrie TenBoom
Tommy Tyson
William
 Willoughby
Al West
J. Rodman
 Williams

Send
Complete
Catalogue

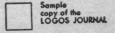

Sample
copy of the
LOGOS JOURNAL

Order blank on previous page

**LOGOS INSTITUTE OF
BIBLICAL STUDIES**

A continuing university without walls
bringing the school to the student
Offering courses in
Biblical Studies
Theological Studies
Historical Studies
Ministry Studies

For further information, write
Registrar
Logos Institute of Biblical Studies
Box 191, Plainfield
New Jersey 07061 U. S. A.